DISCOVER
CANOEING

A complete introduction to open canoeing | **James Weir**

First published in Great Britain 2010 by Pesda Press

Unit 22, Galeri

Doc Victoria

Caernarfon

Gwynedd

LL55 1SQ

ISBN: 978-1-906095-12-3

Printed in Poland, produced by Polska Book.

For my family and friends both on and off the river
for their support and for all the good times.

THE AUTHOR

James Weir

Since discovering open canoeing in the summer of 1988, all James wanted to do was get out on the water and go canoeing. From the early days on the River Thames at Adventure Dolphin in Pangbourne, his enthusiasm for canoeing has taken him to five continents to explore rivers, take part in expeditions and enter competitions. Open canoeing for James started out as a hobby, turned into a lifestyle and is now a profession. In addition to vocational qualifications, he was awarded a sports scholarship to study Adventure Recreation with Sports Science at De Montfort University in Bedford, where he graduated with an honours degree in 2002. James continues to expand the boundaries of his sport and tests and develops products for several of the market leaders in adventure equipment. Presently living and working in the Swiss Alps, he coaches whitewater canoeing and guides rafts at the Kanuschule in Versam. His refreshing approach, experience and competition success make him one of the prominent characters of the sport.

FOREWORD

In my twenty-five years as a canoeist, I have been fortunate to canoe with many of the most amazing paddlers in the world. I have paddled with James in numerous countries and occasionally we have shared the podium after an international competition.

When I first met James he was national open canoe champion representing Great Britain as part of their national freestyle team. Playboating late into the evenings and racing down creeks we bonded as brothers, even though we both desired to be a step higher on the victory platform at the end of the weekend than the other.

James has always had the knack of knowing instinctively where to be in order to enjoy life to the fullest. Two of my favourite memories with James both occurred under full moons: surfing until dawn on the Isar River in Plattling, Germany, and a post dinner paddle in England to Kenneth Grahame's 'Toad Hall' where we "simply messed about in our boats".

Eventually we all grow up and feel the desire to leave something of significance for future generations. With this book James has made it easy for the next generation of aspiring canoeists to rapidly progress and develop their skills. James has combined spectacular photos with easy to follow instructions that help illustrate the fundamentals of canoeing. I hope that you find it helpful and enjoy the opportunity to share many wonderful adventures through canoeing just as James and I have.

Eli Helbert
World Champion Open Canoe Rodeo 1999–2003, 2006
www.thecanoeguru.com

CONTENTS

INTRODUCTION

This is a journey through the sport of open canoeing. It involves a new approach to canoeing: modern ideas and concepts applied to one of the oldest modes of transport known to man. Whether you choose to read this book cover to cover or just look at the photos, I hope you will be motivated to jump up and go canoeing.

After exploring the history of the canoe, advice is provided on preparing for your first canoeing experience, skills and paddle strokes for beginners and experts, skills and tactics for navigating whitewater rapids, Eskimo rolling techniques for whitewater canoes, an explanation of the various competitive disciplines for canoeists and, finally, tips and tricks for expedition canoeing.

Please be careful. Canoeing is not a dangerous sport, but a lack of appropriate safety equipment and training will increase the risk of misadventure in any activity, of which canoeing is no exception. Contact your local shop, coaching provider or club for advice and instruction before venturing out on your own. This book is not a substitute for attending a course run by a professional.

Stay safe and have fun.

James

ACKNOWLEDGEMENTS

Many, many thanks must go to all the people who have gone out of their way to help me realise this book; thanks to the many photographers who have provided beautiful images, to the models who repeated the same thing several times without complaining and to all the companies who provided equipment and advice during the project. Finally thanks to Franco and Peter at Pesda Press for giving me this opportunity and a huge thanks to my family and friends for being there for me when I need them.

Models

Alex Keller, David Lambley, Franziska Biechler, James Weir, Lilli Winter, Pamela Halligey, Susanne Spölmink

Images

Alex Keller – www.alex-keller.net
Andreas Fernekorn – www.deinebilder.com
Beat Rüetimann – www.wavedevil.com
Craig Hill – www.paddlepics.com
Florian Reithmeier – www.bushpaddler.de
Graham Mackereth – www.pyranha.com
James Weir – www.jamesweir.net
Lilli Winter – www.raftinggirls.com
Marc Ornstein
Marilyn Scriver
Markus Leppänen – www.soulboater.blogspot.com
Micha Schomann – www.freestylefoto.org
Michael Cullen – www.canoemuseum.net
Michael Gähwiler – www.whitewater.ch
Michael Neumann – www.kanumagazin.com
Richard Mikosch – www.gesund-bewegen.ch

Sam Ward – www.loveitliveit.co.uk
Steffi Blochwitz – www.nordlichtphoto.com
Susanne Spölmink – www.sanneshome.blogspot.com
Tim Rowland – www.xpaddlers.com

Support

Delta Sportswear – www.delta-sportswear.com
Clothing and accessories for open canoeing.

Esquif Canoes – www.esquif.com
Open canoes for every occasion, from
touring to extreme whitewater.

Gaia Sports – www.gaiasports.com
Environmentally friendly dry bags, airbags
and canoeing accessories.

Kanuschule Versam – www.kanuschule.ch
Open canoe coaching and holidays from beginner to expert.

Kober paddles – www.kober-moll.de
Manufactures of canoe paddles for over 100 years.

Nookie Xtreme Sports Equipment – www.nookie.co.uk
High quality protective clothing and
accessories for whitewater canoeing.

DISCOVERING THE OPEN CANOE

The first open canoes were carved out of tree trunks; this is a Haida dugout canoe from the Queen Charlotte Islands in the Pacific Ocean.

This dugout canoe shows the diversity of shape in early canoe design. The canoe is short and wide and was designed for manoeuvrability instead of straight line speed.

Open canoeing can trace its history back to the first person who sat on a tree trunk to float or paddle across a river or lake many thousands of years ago. Although they didn't know it these people were the pioneers of what is now one of the most popular water sports in the world.

The first active development in the history of canoeing was the dugout canoe. A hull was hollowed out from a tree trunk and paddles were shaped from branches. Paddlers sat inside the canoe and were able to stay dry whilst paddling. The people who invented dugout canoes also invented basic paddle strokes to enable them to paddle and control their canoe as efficiently as possible.

Around the world different cultures developed the canoe in different ways depending on the available local materials and their particular needs; outrigger canoes were developed to enable the canoe to be paddled between Pacific islands and in Canada voyageur canoes were built to transport large loads of animal furs from the wilderness to the market. The open canoe was an important tool for exploration, trading and for hunting. In many developing countries the canoe is still the primary method of transport across water; its simple design and construction allows everybody to access the water, either for fun or out of necessity.

Canoeing for fun

The 19th century saw the start of a new type of popular human activity, leisure; people had time to relax and enjoy themselves and to do something for no reason other than fun. A Scottish lawyer, John 'Rob Roy' MacGregor, pioneered canoeing as a leisure activity in Europe. He designed several canoes and journeyed throughout Europe and Africa with them. In 1866 he formed the world's first canoe club in London and in 1873 it became known as the Royal Canoe Club.

Competitive canoeing started in 1867 with the first canoe regatta at the Canoe Club in London. Sprint canoeing was a demonstration event at the 1924 Paris Olympic Games and was officially included as an Olympic discipline in the 1936 Berlin Olympic Games.

John 'Rob Roy' MacGregor was the pioneer of canoeing as a leisure activity.

Open canoeing has evolved in just over 100 years into one of the most diverse water sports in the world. It is possible to explore lakes and rivers, descend rapids, sail, race, go fishing, surf ocean waves, perform tricks on flat water or whitewater, go birdwatching and most importantly have a lot of fun in your canoe.

Open canoeing is a diverse and popular sport. People all over the world enjoy canoeing every day. These three boys descend one of the smaller rapids on the White Nile in Uganda.

Types of canoe

Open canoes are built in many shapes, sizes and materials. They have evolved independently all over the world to suit the needs of the paddlers and the locally available materials.

Dugout canoe

The first canoes were made from hollowed out logs; these canoes are known as dugouts. Dugout canoes are still in used in many parts of the developing world and their construction is an art form passed down through generations of boat builders. Dugouts vary in size depending on the tree trunk they began as. Dugout canoes can be paddled using a single bladed paddle or propelled using a long wooden pole in shallow water.

General purpose canoe

A general purpose open canoe is the shape that most people imagine a canoe to be. They are typically 16 foot long and made of Royalex plastic, with two seats and a centre thwart. They are symmetrical with the ends turned up slightly at the front and back. A general purpose canoe can be paddled by either one or two people who are sitting or kneeling.

A general purpose open canoe being paddled by two people on a lake; this is a typical open canoeing scene. When paddling in tandem one paddler paddles on the left side and the other on the right using single bladed paddles.

Racing canoe

Canoes designed for sprint or marathon racing are long and thin to reduce water resistance and maximise top speed, and are typically constructed from lightweight composite materials. There are two types of racing canoes: sit and switch and high kneeling. Sit and switch canoes are paddled sitting down and the paddlers frequently swap sides to reduce fatigue. To paddle a high kneeling canoe, the paddler kneels with one foot forward on the hull of the canoe and the other leg bent so that the knee and the top of the foot are resting on the hull. High kneeling canoeists use a long paddle with a large area blade and do not swap sides when paddling. Racing canoes can feel unstable at first, but stability increases with speed.

This sit and switch canoe is made from Kevlar. It has been specially designed for racing and is built from lightweight materials.

Whitewater canoe

Open canoes designed for whitewater use tend to be shorter than a general purpose canoe. The ends are higher, making the canoe look a bit like a banana. Whitewater canoes have airbags added to increase flotation and reduce water intake. A foam saddle and thigh straps increase control over the canoe and allow the paddler to perform an Eskimo roll if they capsize. Whitewater canoes can be fitted with one foam saddle for solo use or two saddles for tandem use. They are normally brightly coloured for safety reasons. Whitewater canoeists kneel in the canoe and use a short single-bladed paddle.

This whitewater canoe is much shorter than a general purpose canoe and features extra fittings to allow for the safe descent of rapids.

Inflatable canoe

Inflatable canoes are easy to recognise. Designed primarily for whitewater use, they are constructed using strong abrasion-resistant rubber. An inflatable canoe is constructed of three parts: the floor and two side tubes. There are two seats that can be easily moved forwards or backwards to adapt the canoe for solo or tandem use. Many inflatable canoes are self bailing: at the back of the canoe on the floor there is a drainage tube to allow any water that enters the canoe to flow out. Inflatable canoes can be paddled sitting or kneeling or by one or two paddlers using single-bladed paddles.

An inflatable canoe for whitewater, symmetrical with dramatic rocker at both ends.

Paddles

A canoe paddle; blade, shaft and T grip.

The first canoeists used trimmed branches to push off the river bed to propel their log canoes along. These poles were not effective in deep water and so one end was widened to increase purchase on the water: the paddle was born. The basic shape of a paddle has remained unchanged since its conception and comprises three parts: the paddle blade, the shaft and a T grip.

Features and their effect

There are eight basic parts that make up an open canoe: the bow, stern, hull, seats, thwarts, yoke, gunwale and deck plates. The bow is the name for the front of the canoe and the stern is the back of the canoe. Most open canoes are symmetrical and therefore the front and the back look the same. A high and rounded bow or stern is an advantage when paddling through waves or rough water as it deflects water away from the canoe. It is a disadvantage when the wind blows, however, because the large area will be caught by the wind making the canoe difficult to control.

A 16-foot general purpose open canoe with wooden gunwales, two seats, a kneeling thwart and a carrying yoke.

Hull

Hull is the term used to refer to the bottom of the canoe; the shape of the hull affects the way in which the canoe reacts and responds. Rounded or displacement hulls, a feature of racing and fast touring canoes, travel through the water with minimal resistance but will have a slightly unstable feel. A flat hull will feel initially much more stable than a rounded hull, but will be trickier to handle in rough water as the hull will roll to remain parallel with the surface of the water. The classic Prospector canoe design has a flat hull. A shallow V hull shape is more stable in rough water than a flat hull. The slight keel effect assists travelling in a straight line but may slip over the water and feel unstable when making tight turns.

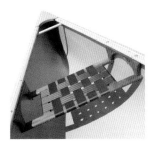

This is a webbing seat. Seat-belt-type webbing has been fixed over a wooden frame.

Seats

Most general purpose canoes are fitted with two seats, one at the front and one at the back. The positioning of these seats allows you to work out which end is the front of the canoe. The front seat is closer to the middle of the canoe than the back seat. If you find that you have very little space for your legs, you are probably sitting on the back seat facing the back of the canoe. Seats come in three main types: a moulded plastic seat, a wood frame with seat belt webbing or a wooden frame with woven cane. A plastic seat is robust and the best choice for club or rental canoes. They are the heaviest type of seat and uncomfortable to sit on facing the wrong way, making them unsuitable for solo canoeing. A wooden framed seat with webbing is fairly robust and is easy to repair if damaged; they are also lightweight. The major disadvantage of the wooden frame with webbing is that it takes a long time to dry, leading to some discomfort for the paddler. A wooden framed seat with cane is the least robust of the three variations, but also the lightest and very quick drying. For a careful paddler, wooden framed with cane seats are robust enough to last the lifetime of the canoe. However, they are difficult to repair if damaged.

On the right is a carrying yoke; note the cut-out for your neck. On the left is a kneeling thwart.

Yokes and thwarts

Thwart and yoke are terms used to describe the horizontal braces that are fixed widthways across the canoe. Most open canoes feature wooden thwarts and yokes although canoes with lightweight aluminium thwarts also exist. Thwarts are added to the canoe to improve the rigidity of the hull. A yoke is a specially crafted thwart designed to make carrying a canoe on your shoulders as comfortable as possible. The cut-out in the middle is for your neck and the bumps on either side are designed to rest on your shoulders. A yoke should be fitted in the middle of the canoe so it will be perfectly balanced when carried on the shoulders. A kneeling thwart is installed in a canoe to make solo paddling more comfortable. They are usually installed between the yoke and back seat.

Gunwales

The black plastic edge on the top of this canoe is known as the gunwale; it helps to keep the canoe rigid and can be used to fix thwarts into the canoe.

Gunwales are added to an open canoe to increase hull rigidity. Fixed to the top edge of the open canoe, they provide a solid framework when combined with thwarts. Most general purpose canoes are fitted with plastic gunwales which are tough and require no maintenance. The disadvantages of plastic gunwales compared to wood is that they are heavy and, if broken, the entire length of gunwale must be replaced (but plastic gunwales are very robust).

Wooden gunwales are the choice of the connoisseur; a canoe with all wood fittings is much lighter and more beautiful than one with plastic fittings. The beauty comes at a price, however. Wooden gunwales are more expensive than plastic ones and must be regularly oiled or varnished to preserve their strength and appearance. Wooden gunwales are more prone to damage than their plastic alternative, but are easier to repair with basic woodworking skills.

A deck plate.

Deck plate

Deck plate is the name given to the small plastic or wooden triangular feature at each end of the canoe. The deck plates are designed to protect the ends of the canoe and the ends of the gunwales. They complement the gunwales and are made from the same material. Plastic deck plates often feature a combined carrying handle; wooden deck plates will have a separate wooden carrying handle.

Rocker

Rocker is a term used to describe the height difference between the middle of the canoe on the hull and the point where the hull becomes the bow or stern of the canoe, a 15cm difference is considered to be a lot of rocker. Rocker is added to a design to maximise the turning ability of the canoe and to improve dryness when the canoe is paddled through waves. Increasing the rocker makes a canoe harder to paddle in a straight line, reduces the potential top speed and will make the canoe trickier to control in wind. A canoe with pronounced rocker is suitable for whitewater use and a canoe with zero rocker is more suited to flat water racing or touring.

Chine

Chine is a term used to describe the angle between the side and the hull of the canoe. A flat hulled canoe with vertical sides is said to have hard chines and a canoe with a rounded hull has soft chines. The chine or the edge of the canoe can be used by advanced paddlers to grip the water to stop the canoe slipping when turning at high speed. Racing canoes have very soft chines and whitewater freestyle canoes have hard chines.

Tumblehome and flare

Tumblehome and flare are terms used to describe the angle of the sides of the canoe. When the gunwales are wider than the hull, the canoe is said to have flare. Flare helps to keep water out of the canoe when paddling through waves or rapids. Tumblehome is the opposite of flare: the sides of the canoe curve in towards the gunwales, the hull of the canoe is therefore wider than the gunwales. Adding tumblehome to a canoe will make it easier to paddle as the canoeist need not reach so far out to place the paddle in the water.

The canoe on the left is wider at the bottom than the top: this is tumblehome. The canoe on the right is wider at the top than the bottom: this is flare.

Extra features for whitewater canoes

Whitewater canoes have extra fittings for performance and safety. Airbags should be added to all canoes used on whitewater. The space taken up by the airbags reduces the amount of water that can enter the canoe, keeping the canoe as light as possible. The additional flotation provided by the airbags also makes it easier to rescue the canoe after a capsize and less susceptible to damage as it floats down the river. Airbags should be securely fixed into the canoe using deck lashing and anchor straps. An airbag that is not fixed to the canoe may break free under pressure and the canoe will fill with water.

An airbag in a whitewater canoe: note that the lashing to hold the airbag in place extends over the airbag and down to the hull to keep the airbag fixed into the end of the canoe.

On the left is a bulkhead-style saddle system with thigh straps; ideal for advanced paddlers who require complete control. On the right is a pedestal saddle with a double strap system; much easier to adjust and it's easy to exit in the event of a capsize.

A foam saddle is glued into the middle of the canoe to provide a stable seating position. Foot rests and knee pads can also be added to increase comfort. To improve control, whitewater paddlers often add a foam bulkhead over the knees and quick release thigh straps to secure themselves into the canoe. The advantage of the saddle seating system is that it fixes the paddlers into the canoe and they are able to control the canoe much better. Saddle seats are also very comfortable when set up correctly.

Materials

Wood

The first open canoes were made from wood, when craftsmen hollowed out tree trunks to make dugout canoes. Wood is still popular and can be used in many different ways to make open canoes. Lengths of bark from birch trees can be sewn together with tree roots, stretched over a wooden frame and then waterproofed with resin. Thin strips of wood can be used to build very beautiful wood strip canoes; the strips of wood are glued together over a

A beautiful lightweight wood strip canoe for the connoisseur. Photo: Canadian Canoe Museum.

wooden frame and then waterproofed using epoxy or polyester resin. The finished canoe is lifted off the frame and then gunwales and internal fittings can be added. Planks of wood can also be used to build canoes using a similar technique. The planks are normally sewn together with wire or strong thread and then covered with resin to waterproof and protect the hull.

The primary advantage of a wooden canoe is that it is light; they are also reasonably strong and often very beautiful. Wooden canoes need to be looked after, stored in a sheltered place and regularly maintained, as a neglected wooden canoe will deteriorate very quickly. Wood is a good choice for careful owners.

Composite

Materials such as glass fibre, Kevlar and carbon fibre can be laid up in a mould and combined with epoxy or polyester resin to form a canoe hull. Modern thermoplastic composites such as Twin-tex can be vacuum packed then cooked in an oven to create strong and lightweight canoes. Early glass fibre open canoes were heavy but recent advances allow much lighter hulls to be built.

This whitewater freestyle canoe is made from Kevlar. It is lightweight and strong, perfect for competition use.

The principal advantage of composites is that very lightweight and stiff hulls can be built. Canoes built specifically for competition use are often made from composites. The main disadvantage of a composite canoe is its strength. If well looked after, a composite canoe will last a long time but they are easier to damage than a wooden or plastic canoe; they are, however, the easiest to repair if damaged. Twin-tex is difficult to repair. The technology to repair the material exists but is not readily available and a damaged canoe must be professionally repaired. A composite canoe is good for those paddlers looking for an extra competitive advantage.

Royalex

Royalex and Royalite are two similar materials more commonly known as ABS. Royalite has fewer laminate layers making it lighter but also slightly weaker than Royalex. Sheets of Royalex and Royalite are heated then moulded to the shape of a canoe hull. The combination of processes and materials produces an excellent canoe that is highly resistant to abrasion and heavy impacts. The Royalex material has incredible structural memory, a canoe can be bent (even folded in two) and it will pop back into shape with minimal permanent damage. Most open canoes produced are made from Royalex.

Royalex canoes are much stronger than composite canoes and lighter than plastic canoes. Royalite is noticeably lighter than Royalex but also slightly less robust. Royalite canoes are chosen when weight is more important than strength; touring canoes and solo canoes are often made of Royalite. Royalex is a good choice of material for everybody. Even a badly looked after Royalex canoe will last for years and can survive a great deal of mistreatment.

Plastic

Plastic can also be used to mould open canoe hulls. Small plastic pellets are added to a mould which is then spun around in a huge oven to coat the inside of the mould with liquid plastic. The canoe is then allowed to cool until it can be removed from the mould.

A Royalex canoe. Note the different layers of Royalex sandwiched between the wooden gunwales: two thinner layers of ABS on each side and an epoxy-soaked foam core.

A small whitewater canoe. Plastic can be used to mould complex shapes which are difficult to make in other materials.

Open canoes made of plastic are very strong but comparatively heavy. Plastic is not as rigid as other materials and this can lead to the hull flexing slightly in the middle, an effect known as 'oil canning'. Often used for whitewater canoes, the main advantage of plastic is the price. A plastic hull is much cheaper than a Royalex, wooden or composite hull in the same shape. Plastic is an ideal material for paddlers looking for good value or a strong whitewater canoe, as smaller whitewater canoes do not suffer from oil canning.

Responsibilities of an open canoeist

A good open canoeist is also a conscientious one. There are three areas I'm going to stress: safety, the environment, and fun.

Being safe is important. Always wear your buoyancy aid and don't go canoeing alone; it is safer and more fun with friends.

To really enjoy yourself, you and your canoeing buddies need to feel safe. Safety is about identifying and avoiding hazards and reducing risks. If you are new to open canoeing, enrol in a course with a qualified coach; you will progress quicker and more comfortably with professional coaching. Prepare thoroughly for your canoeing experience: dress appropriately for the weather and water temperature and check that your canoe and equipment are in good working order. Tell somebody where you are going, what you are planning to do and when you expect to return. If anything goes wrong they will be able to alert the relevant authorities. Plan to keep within the limits of your ability as biting off more than you can chew is the most common cause of misadventure.

Planet Earth is a great place to play. We should all do our best to preserve it.

Planet Earth is our home and our playground and we should do everything in our power to protect the natural world from unnecessary damage and pollution. Canoeing is, generally speaking, an environmentally friendly sport. A canoe is human powered and can travel across water without leaving any trace of having been there. Responsible canoeists limit their impact on the environment by taking their rubbish with them to dispose of correctly and, where possible, tidying up any rubbish they find on their journey. When walking to or from the waters edge follow marked footpaths and take care not to break or damage vegetation when carrying your canoe. Repair or recycle worn out equipment instead of simply throwing it out; you will be saving money as well as the planet.

Happy canoeists are good canoeists so never, ever forget to have fun.

Fun is a very important factor for open canoeing; if you are not enjoying yourself then something is not right. A happy and re-laxed paddler is less prone to injury, better prepared to learn and can concentrate 100% on getting the most out of their canoeing experience. Every paddler is responsible for enjoying themselves and making sure their paddling companions are also enjoying themselves. If somebody is struggling then help them out; if they are cold offer them a warm drink or a woolly hat. Open canoeing is a great sport and the more people who participate, the greater the sport will become. When out and about with your canoe enjoy yourself – there is no better advertisement for the sport than a group of happy people safely cruising down a river.

BEFORE THE WATER

Ready to go open canoeing.

Choosing suitable equipment for open canoeing is one of the most important decisions you will make. Uncomfortable or unsuitable equipment will hinder progress and not work with you to help make the most of your day. There are many different designs of canoes, paddles and clothing for open canoeing, each item with its own particular forte. Your aim is to choose the equipment that best suits your needs. Before you can make this decision you need to assess your needs. Do you require a canoe that is suitable for going on a picnic or for whitewater, a paddle for touring or sprint racing?

Take your time to choose the most suitable equipment for your needs; a paddle that is too long or too short will challenge progress.

Information on equipment can be gained from many different sources: your own knowledge and research and that of your peers; manufacturers' advertising; and from your local canoe retailer. This chapter will explain how different features affect the performance of equipment and how to apply this knowledge to choosing suitable equipment for your needs.

Every canoeist should be water confident and be able to swim. A buoyancy aid will help you to float in water but unsuitable clothes and shoes can hinder attempts to move quickly in the water. All canoeists should be able to comfortably swim at least twenty-five metres while wearing their canoeing clothing, shoes and buoyancy aid.

All canoeists should be able to swim at least 25 metres wearing their canoeing clothes. Practise swimming in your canoeing kit – it's fun!

Software

Buoyancy aids

The most important item for every canoeist is the buoyancy aid. You can go canoeing without a buoyancy aid but you shouldn't, safety equipment reduces risk. For many paddlers a buoyancy aid is the first item of canoeing specific equipment they buy. The most important factors to consider when choosing a buoyancy aid to borrow or buy is that it fits correctly and that it is in good condition. A correctly fitting buoyancy aid should comfortably hug your body, allow complete freedom of movement and be comfortable to put on, take off and wear. A buoyancy aid should be a bright colour or feature panels of brightly coloured material and, ideally, feature panels of reflective material on the shoulder straps.

A correctly fitting buoyancy aid is essential for canoeing. Before taking to the water, check that everyone's buoyancy aid fits correctly.

Although better than no buoyancy aid at all, a badly fitting buoyancy aid (whether too small or too big) provides a false sense of security and will hinder movement when paddling and swimming. A buoyancy aid that is too big may ride up over the head when you are in the water, reducing your ability to see and your visibility to others as you will float lower in the water. In extreme cases, you may fall out of the buoyancy aid completely. A buoyancy aid that is too small may not provide sufficient buoyancy to float you in the water and may not fasten properly.

Buoyancy aids suitable for open canoeing can be divided into two general categories: the zip-up jacket style and the over-the-head vest style. Many paddlers prefer the zip-up jacket style as they find it easier to put on and take off (this is particularly true if you wear a drysuit). Others support the theory that because the vest style is simpler, it is therefore less likely to fail (there is no zip to

(Left) a vest-style buoyancy aid; a simple design but some paddlers find it harder to get on and off than (right) a zip-up, jacket-style buoyancy aid.

break, for instance). Competition paddlers usually wear vest-style buoyancy aids as they are slightly less bulky, allowing greater freedom of movement. Most buoyancy aids feature several adjustment straps: a waist belt; two shoulder adjustment straps; and two straps under the arms to help you achieve the best fit.

⚠ Buoyancy aids designed for whitewater may also feature a chest/safety harness. If you do not know how to correctly use the chest harness system you should remove it and store it in a safe place. The chest harness is not necessary to achieve a good fit and can be dangerous when misused.

The chest harness system featured on whitewater buoyancy aids should only be used by paddlers who have been trained to use them. Note the yellow quick release toggle.

Pockets are a practical feature, a place to store a few essential items close to hand. Do not carry anything unnecessary in your pockets as bulky pockets will hinder your ability to climb back into the canoe after a capsize. Unnecessary items in your pockets may slow you down when reaching for something useful; the last thing you want in your hand when reaching for your knife is a muesli bar. Hunger can wait thirty seconds, a friend tangled in a rope underwater cannot.

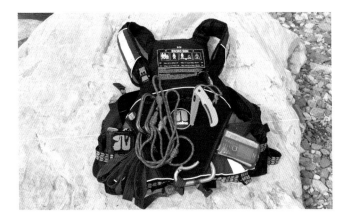

These are the items I always carry in my buoyancy aid pockets: a knife, sling, whistle, karabiners, prussic loops (for hauling on ropes) and a mobile phone.

A hydration system in your buoyancy aid will allow hands-free drinking while paddling.

Some buoyancy aids feature a pocket on the back to house a drinks system. A bladder sits in the pocket and a pipe runs to the shoulder strap with a bite valve to allow hands-free drinking. We all dream of paddling rivers clean enough to drink, but sadly this is often not the case. Keeping hydrated is key to performing well in any activity.

Shoes

Good shoes are essential equipment for all canoeists. Canoeing in bare feet may be a pleasant experience in warm conditions but increases the risk of injuring your feet. For whitewater canoeing, warm supportive shoes or boots with a good grip should always

You can wear neoprene socks inside your shoes to add warmth and ankle support.

be worn. Whitewater canoeing without shoes is dangerous, not only for yourself but for your fellow paddlers. You need to be able to move confidently and quickly across steep and slippery rock if the need arises.

Three types of river shoe. Neoprene boots are light, warm and provide moderate ankle support. River trainers are very comfy and quick drying, but provide no ankle support. Canyoning boots are hard wearing, give superb ankle support and are warm, but they are heavier than the other options and take longer to dry.

Most trainers are suitable for canoeing as they are lightweight, quick drying and have a rubber sole which will grip wet rock. Avoid leather shoes and heavy hiking boots. Sports sandals are popular for warm weather canoeing – they are, however, not very comfortable to wear when kneeling, are potentially more likely to snag than trainers, and look 'uncool' when worn with socks, neoprene or otherwise. Sandals provide no ankle support when you slip and twist your ankle on uneven ground. For cold water and weather, wear neoprene socks inside your trainers; I find the combination of neoprene socks and trainers is better for open canoeing than neoprene boots. Canyoning boots are favoured by many whitewater canoeists; robust, warm, with a good grip and support, canyoning boots tick all the boxes for good canoeing shoes.

Good canoeing shoes should grip even on wet and slippery rock.

Clothing

Wearing the right clothing will enhance your day. Cold and wet paddlers do not have as much fun as warm, dry paddlers.

Different weather conditions require different degrees of protective clothing. Fleece and shorts; fleece and semi-dry shell jacket and trousers with sun visor; drysuit over a base layer with warm helmet.

Consider the water temperature and weather forecast. Shorts and a T-shirt may be appropriate for a sunny summer afternoon cruise on your local lake but are completely unsuitable for a winter day paddle on whitewater river. Wearing several layers of clothing is a good principle when dressing for a canoeing adventure.

The **base layer** is the most important layer, either worn on its own on a warm day or under the insulating and shell layers when cold or wet. Base layer thermals should ideally be made from a synthetic material that has a skin-tight fit to the body but is stretchy enough to allow your full range of movement. The purpose of the base layer is to wick perspiration away from the skin, to keep the body warm and dry.

An **insulating layer** will keep the body warm by trapping warm air between it and the base layer. Man-made fleece is the most popular choice, since fleece clothing is easily available, lightweight and quick drying. Getting to know your body will help you to decide how many fleece layers to wear to stay warm. Many paddlers will leave out the insulation layer if the weather is not too cold and wear just the base and shell layers. Wind- and water-repellent fleece jackets are also good for gusty or showery days.

(Left) a base thermal layer and middle fleece layer. (Right) a breathable, waterproof and windproof shell layer.

The outer or **shell layer** will finish the set. A waterproof and windproof barrier to keep the elements out, most shell layers are made from breathable fabrics that allow sweat to evaporate away from the body. Canoeing-specific shell layers fall into two categories: semi-dry and dry. Semi-dry trousers and jackets have simple adjustable neoprene seals on the ankles, wrists and neck. These are comfortable but will not keep the water out if submerged underwater. For most open canoeing, a semi-dry shell layer is the ideal choice. Paddling jackets with hoods are well suited to open canoeing as they will keep the head dry and out of the wind.

LATEX SEALS CAN BE TRICKY TO PUT ON AND TAKE OFF AND UNCOMFORTABLE TO WEAR FOR LONG PERIODS OF TIME, BUT PROVIDE THE ONLY REAL SOLUTION TO KEEPING DRY WHEN IN THE WATER.

When venturing onto cold water, consider a 'dry' shell layer. Ankle, wrist and neck seals made from latex rubber will keep out water even when submerged underwater. Separate dry trousers and cags are available as well as all-in-one drysuits (which are considered by many whitewater canoeists to be the ultimate shell layer).

A separate shell jacket and trouser combination will allow you to adapt to changing weather conditions and they are more easily replaced (canoeists tend to wear out trousers quicker than jackets, from kneeling and portaging over rough ground). But separates may be less watertight when submerged (normally badly fitting combinations; a good combination will keep you dry).

On the other hand a good all-in-one drysuit should guarantee to keep you dry but has a few disadvantages. Unless it has a relief zip, you'll need to undress to answer the call of nature which can be unpleasant if it is cold or raining. You may need a friend to help zip you into your drysuit if the entry zip is across the shoulders.

Protecting your head

A hat will protect your head: a woolly hat for cold weather and a wide-brimmed hat for hot and sunny weather. Most of your body heat is lost through your head. If you feel yourself becoming cold, put on a fleece or woolly hat to help retain body heat.

A wide-brimmed hat will help shade the face and back of the neck from harmful UV rays.

A woolly hat will help the body to retain warmth on a cold day.

Prolonged exposure to strong sunshine can be very damaging for human skin; even short exposure to direct sunshine can cause sunburn. Protect yourself from the harmful UV rays by wearing a sun hat or visor when the weather is fine.

A correctly fitting helmet is one of the most important pieces of safety equipment for whitewater canoeing.

A helmet should be taken on every journey on which you are likely to find moving water. The purpose of a helmet is to protect your head in the event of a bump and it can only do this if it fits correctly. A helmet that slips forwards over the eyes or back off the head may not protect you in the event of a collision, and may leave the vulnerable areas of the forehead, back of the head and temples exposed. Helmets specifically designed for canoeing are best as they will have passed a safety test for watersport helmets. A ski or cycling helmet will protect the head to a certain extent but will not be ideal. The addition of a peak or visor will shield the eyes from sun, improving visibility and reducing the risk of eye damage from prolonged exposure to direct sunlight. A helmet can also provide valuable warmth on cold days.

 Your head is not only at risk when canoeing: many people slip when walking over wet rock or uneven ground to inspect rapids. Keep your helmet on at all times. It can only protect you if you are wearing it.

When outfitted with appropriate equipment, the only thing left to do is enjoy yourself.

Aim to wear the best clothing, footwear and helmet possible for you. Although you will be pleased to save money in the shop by buying a cheaper product, you may regret it later on the river when you are uncomfortable, cold or wet.

Hardware

Paddles

Paddles of all shapes and sizes can be made from various materials, each with their own particular advantages. Most general purpose canoe paddles are made from plastic and aluminium. Touring paddles are generally made from wood, whitewater and competition paddles are generally made from composite materials such as glass fibre. A general purpose canoe paddle will feature a flat, rectangular, square-tipped blade made of plastic, an aluminium shaft and a plastic T grip. These paddles are reasonably light, robust and cheap and can be used for every type of canoeing.

A selection of canoe paddles. From left to right: a carbon fibre competition paddle, a wooden touring paddle, a fibreglass whitewater paddle and a plastic and aluminium general purpose paddle.

Wooden paddles are the choice of the traditionalist: the first canoe paddles were carved from wood and the designs have changed little. Wood paddles are warm to hold on cold days, soft to paddle with and are the choice of many touring canoeists. Touring paddle designs can be divided into two groups: the **beaver tail** and the **otter tail** style paddle. **Beaver tail** paddles are flat bladed, rounded at the bottom and about the same width at the widest point as a square-tipped paddle. They are good general purpose paddles; the wide blade allows a quick energy transfer from paddle to water, even when only half the paddle blade is in water. **Otter tail** paddles are also known as deep water touring paddles. They feature long narrow blades which are rounded at the end. Otter tail paddles have a much slower energy transfer because the long blade must be completely submerged before most of the blade area is covered. This slow energy transfer is very gentle on the arms and shoulders and therefore ideal for paddlers on long tours who do not wish to tire themselves out too quickly.

From left to right: a beaver tail paddle, a square-tipped paddle and an otter tail paddle. On long journeys or tours many paddlers use comfortable wooden paddles to reduce stress on muscles and tendons.

Touring paddles usually feature a much smaller and more rounded T grip, allowing it to be palmed in the hand as the paddle is moved through the water. Wooden paddles that are used for whitewater feature a squared-tipped paddle blade, similar to a general purpose paddle. They are often reinforced on the blade with fibreglass and on the tip of the blade with epoxy resin. Wooden paddles need to be looked after by regular oiling or varnishing.

For whitewater canoeing, stronger, lighter and more responsive composite paddles are favoured by many canoeists.

Whitewater and competition paddles are generally made from glass or carbon fibre. They are lightweight and strong and most tend to feature a curved blade. The curve in the paddle blade grips the water better, allowing more powerful paddle strokes. The composite construction makes the paddle much stiffer so energy transfer from the muscles through the paddle to the water and feedback from the water to the paddler is more efficient. Many recreational paddlers find composite paddles uncomfortable to use as the stiffness puts unnecessary stress and strain on the joints and muscles. Conversely, competitive paddlers are often frustrated by the wasted energy and lack of response from wooden or plastic paddles. Composite paddles are the strongest and, well made, will survive all but the most severe stresses.

Choosing the correct length of paddle is important. A paddle that is too long or too short will make paddling inefficient and uncomfortable. There are two rules that can be applied to select a paddle of an appropriate length:

For a basic sizing rule, a paddle should be slightly shorter than the height to your chin. This technique will measure the total length of paddle and its suitability for your height. It works best with general purpose paddles and for paddlers who will spend most of their time sitting in the canoe.

For a better sizing rule kneel down as if you were kneeling in a canoe, set the paddle upside down with the T grip on the ground, and hold the paddle just below its neck (the join between the paddle blade and the shaft). Your arm should be horizontal or slightly lower at the hand end when you have a correctly sized paddle. This technique measures the length of the paddle shaft and can be used to size paddles with unusually shaped blades.

Two rules for sizing your paddle:
(1) just shorter than the height of your chin when standing.
(2) kneeling down to measure the paddle shaft length will ensure a near-perfect solution for paddlers who kneel the majority of the time in their canoe.

Canoes

At first glance most open canoes look very similar. The key to choosing a suitable canoe is to identify and understand how different design features affect the performance of the canoe. For many, the colour is an important deciding factor; a recreational canoeist will want to use a brightly-coloured canoe for safety reasons and a canoe fisherman may choose a more subtle colour to blend in with the environment.

A Prospector design open canoe being paddled tandem on flat water.

WHEN CHOOSING A CANOE TO PADDLE CHECK THAT IT IS IN A GOOD STATE OF REPAIR. THE HULL IS INTACT AND WITHOUT ANY SERIOUS DAMAGE, THE SEATS AND YOKE ARE SECURELY BOLTED TO THE GUNWALES AND THAT ANY ADDITIONAL BUOYANCY IS CORRECTLY FITTED AND FULLY INFLATED.

A canoe can be identified by the length, the rocker and the hull shape. Sixteen foot is the standard length for a general purpose open canoe, whereas expedition and racing canoes tend to be longer. Racing canoes feature low sides and narrower width while expedition canoes are wider with higher sides to increase the freeboard. Canoes shorter than sixteen foot that look similar to general purpose canoes may be designed for solo paddling or for tandem crews of children. If both ends of the canoe turn up (making the canoe look banana shaped) it is said to have a lot of rocker and is designed for whitewater use. A canoe that is entirely flat along the gunwales will be designed for flat water racing.

Try out as many different canoes as possible during your first canoeing experiences. See how different hull designs affect the performance of the canoe. When choosing a canoe try as many types as you can until you find a canoe that complements your paddling style.

Transporting your canoe

Although a perfect craft travelling on water, a canoe can be unwieldy to transport on land. Carrying a canoe on land can be done in pairs using the carrying handles at each end or alone using the portage yoke in the middle of the canoe. For long distances over level ground a portage trolley can be used. Before attempting to lift a canoe, be sure you have properly warmed up. Lifting and carrying a canoe can cause injuries if done improperly.

(Left) a portage trolley is an easy way to transport your canoe over flat and even ground. Photo: Michael Gähwiler (Right) two adults can safely and easily carry a canoe on opposite sides, at the front and back.

Carrying a canoe in a pair is a simple exercise – one paddler at each end and on opposite sides. Use the carrying handles and swap sides at regular intervals to prevent straining one side of the body excessively. The correct technique for lifting the canoe is to keep your back straight and bend your legs as you squat down to pick up the canoe. Keep your arms and back straight as you stand up.

Carrying your canoe solo using the portage yoke is a surprisingly comfortable way a transporting the canoe; it is also much easier than a two person carry over uneven terrain. Once the yoke is on your shoulders and the canoe balanced it is comfortable and secure. The trick is to lift the canoe into that position without twisting your back.

Solo carry using a portage yoke. Photo: Michael Gähwiler

To lift a canoe onto your shoulders start in the middle of the canoe with one person on each side. Lift the canoe up together and then transfer the weight so that only one person is supporting the canoe. The carrier can then position himself under the yoke and take the weight. To lift the canoe back down, follow the same process in reverse.

Before carrying your canoe along a new portage trail, first walk it while carrying your paddles and dry bags. Discover the easiest route to bring your canoe along when you make the second journey along the trail.

Canoes and cars

Most paddlers will need to transport their canoe by vehicle at some point. Learning how to safely and securely fasten your canoe to a roof rack or trailer is a key skill for every paddler to learn. As a basic rule, canoes are best transported upside down with the gunwales sitting on the roof racks or trailer bars. An upside-down canoe is more aerodynamic and will not fill with water if it rains. Before loading your canoe onto the roof rack, check that the roof rack is correctly secured to the vehicle.

Transporting your canoe on land should not be a struggle; do it in style. Specifically designed roof rack straps are the easiest method of securing your canoe to your roof rack. Note the red roof bar pad.

Tie the canoe down using roof rack straps or lengths of rope. If you choose to use rope, be sure you know your knots. On long journeys, or for extra peace of mind, tie the front and back of the canoe down to the emergency towing eyelets on the vehicle using lengths of rope. When travelling long distances or over bumpy ground make regular checks to be sure the canoe is still firmly attached. The addition of roof bar pads to your roof rack will reduce any potential for damage to the gunwales of the canoe during transport (this is especially important for canoes with wooden gunwales).

Access

Access rules and rights vary from country to country and place to place. One rule is common: before venturing out onto the water, find out if you need permission to paddle or to use the path or road to the put-in. Water can be classified into several categories: tidal, public rights of navigation and privately owned waterways.

Before getting onto the water, responsible canoeists should check if they need permission to paddle there. Canoeists have permission to paddle most navigable inland waterways.

Tidal water, the sea and estuaries up to the spring tide high water mark can be paddled by all. The sea belongs to everybody; no licence or permission is required. The sea is a challenging environment for all and certainly not a suitable place for novice or inexperienced paddlers.

Not all people are happy to see canoeists enjoying the water. Photograph: SCA

Public rights of navigation on inland waterways allow canoeists to access the water at specific put-in and take-out points and journey between these points. Registration or a licence is often required. The profits from the licence fees are used to look after the local environment and maintain access points. Be prepared to share the water with anglers, pleasure cruisers and rowers and respect each others needs and interests.

Most waterways are owned privately and have rules on access imposed on them. Some generous landowners are prepared to allow access for all providing the environment is respected; others selfishly deny access to their land and water. Many privately owned waterways have access restricted to certain times of the year, e.g. hunting and fishing groups may only allow access in their off season. To gain respect canoeists should obey access agreements where they exist and act pleasantly and considerately at all times to all people regardless of their attitude to us.

Wherever you paddle you should always leave everything as you found it. Take all rubbish with you, close gates behind you and cause as little environmental damage as possible. "Leave nothing but footprints; take nothing but photos."

The Grand Canyon on the Colorado River in America is a good example of an access agreement-limited river. It is one of the most visually spectacular and physically demanding river trips possible with an open canoe. The American National Park Service limits numbers of access permits per year to reduce environmental damage to the canyon and to ensure all visitors enjoy an experience of a lifetime. A lottery system awards permits on a random basis to paddlers who pass all the relevant prerequisites.

The Grand Canyon is one of the most famous access-controlled rivers in the world. Only paddlers who have a permit are allowed to paddle down through the Canyon.

Research whether you are permitted to paddle a river or lake; ask your local club or canoe shop or search for information on the internet. If you can't find any information try to contact the land owner. If you are unable to discover any information on the access situation, you have two options: give up and go somewhere else or go ahead and paddle as pioneers of a new stretch of water. If you believe that you have discovered a new stretch of water to paddle, take photographs and record any relevant information about put-ins, take-outs and any hazards along the way.

Warm up and cool down

Before any kind of strenuous activity a warm-up will reduce the likelihood of injury; canoeing is no exception. You should warm up before lifting your canoe down from the roof rack and carrying it to the water's edge. When you have finished canoeing, you should cool down to prevent cramps and muscle stiffness and to relax.

To prepare your body for an activity you should only stretch very gently after you have warmed your muscles with light exercise. Gentle stretching will help you to use your normal full range of movement. If you feel the need to increase your flexibility, you should consider taking up yoga or Pilates as a separate activity.

A few minutes jogging will raise the heart beat, warm muscles, lubricate joints and prepare the body for movement.

A warm-up should be completed in two stages. First, jogging or briskly walking will warm the muscles and raise the pulse. Continue for five minutes or until your body feels physically warmer and your pulse rate has increased.

Next do some gentle stretching to prepare the muscles and whole body for the range of movement that paddling will demand. Start with your neck and move down through the body until you have stretched all the major muscle groups.

Rotating your shoulders gently will warm up the muscles. Stretching your wrists and your forearms will help prevent tendon problems. Side stretches will prepare your torso muscles. And stretch your legs to prepare the muscles for kneeling; you'll also need your legs for canoeing.

A thorough warm-up routine should take between fifteen and twenty minutes and will improve performance by preparing muscles for action and focusing the mind on the paddling to come.

COOLING DOWN AFTER EXERCISE IS JUST AS IMPORTANT AS WARMING UP IN PREVENTING INJURY AND HELPING THE BODY TO RECOVER.

Cooling down after paddling is just as important as warming up to prevent injury. Cool down in a similar way to warming up. Gentle exercise (such as jogging for five minutes, becoming gradually slower then followed by relaxed stretching) will reduce the concentrated salts in the bloodstream that cause muscle cramps, reduce the adrenalin levels in the blood and help the heart to gradually return to its resting rate.

ON THE WATER

Once all preparations have been completed get out on the water and enjoy yourself.

Once you are prepared there is only one thing left to do: get out on the water and have a go. The strokes and techniques covered in the basics section will enable you and a friend to get out on the water, move your canoe in all directions and enjoy yourself on flat water. The intermediate section introduces slightly more challenging paddle strokes; it also covers techniques needed to paddle your canoe solo. The advanced section includes strokes that will make you look and paddle like a pro; many of these strokes rely on the subtleties of the edge of the canoe and the angle of the paddle blade. Logically, you should not attempt to learn the advanced paddle strokes until you have mastered the basic and intermediate strokes. Good luck and remember to have fun.

Getting ready

The first skill to learn is climbing aboard your canoe. Most aspiring canoeists should be able to manage this without instruction. There are however a few things to consider. Search out the easiest place to climb into your canoe. A one-metre drop from the side to the water or higher is liable to present problems as it will be tricky to step into the canoe and to hold onto the side once you

are aboard. When you are putting onto a river with any kind of current or flow, always do so with the front of the canoe pointing upstream. The reason for this is simple: if there is anything floating down with the current you will be able to see it before it causes you any difficulty. Imagine climbing into your canoe as a log floats downstream, bumping into the back of your canoe and causing you to capsize – not the ideal start. Always get into your canoe with the front facing upstream.

First the back paddler climbs in and then the front paddler, both holding onto their paddles. Once both paddlers are seated and ready, off you go.

The back paddler should climb into the canoe first, bringing their paddle with them, then sit or kneel in position and hold onto the side. The front paddler can then climb aboard. The reason that the back paddler gets in first is because it is easier for the back paddler to see what the front paddler is doing and react quicker in case of anything surprising occurring. If the front paddler gets in first they must either turn round to watch or just rely on the feeling of the canoe, both of which are tricky for beginners.

Sitting and kneeling are the two most common ways to position yourself in a canoe.

Once in the canoe it is time to decide how and where to position yourself. Most canoes come fitted with seats (one in the front and one in the back) and sitting in the middle of the seat is a good start for learning to canoe. Once you have decided where to position yourself, you can consider how to position yourself, i.e. sitting or kneeling down. There is no prescribed right or wrong answer to this question; do whatever is most comfortable for you. Kneeling has the advantage of lowering your centre of gravity, thus making you more stable and allowing for a better feeling for the canoe underneath you. However, sitting is found by many to be far more comfortable over an extended period of time.

 Experiment by positioning yourself in the canoe in as many different ways as you can think of: try sitting, kneeling, half kneeling and standing. Each style has advantages and disadvantages; the key is being familiar with all of them and applying them in the appropriate situations.

Trimming your canoe

Trimming the canoe correctly for the prevailing weather and water conditions is the secret to successful, efficient and trouble-free canoeing. It is all about where you place the weight (the paddlers) in the canoe. An open canoe will pivot about its heaviest point, generally the back. If you intend to paddle into a head wind with the front of the canoe lighter than the back, the wind will push the front of the canoe round, pivoting about the back and leaving you facing the wrong way. Trimming the canoe so it is slightly front heavy will prevent this and enable you to paddle forwards in a straight line as easily as possible. For a tail wind, you should place your weight slightly to the back of the canoe. Although the canoe is more affected by trim during reasonably strong wind, it is easy to experiment in relatively light wind to find the advantage of correctly trimming your canoe.

TRY PADDLING INTO THE WIND BACK HEAVY AND THEN TRY FRONT HEAVY; YOU WILL FEEL THE ADVANTAGE OF CORRECT TRIM.

In the first photo the canoe is trimmed normally when both paddlers sit in their seats and the weight is evenly distributed. In the second photo the canoe is trimmed front heavy for a head wind; in the third it is trimmed back heavy for a tail wind.

The paddle

Holding the canoe paddle correctly will make the difference between a productive day on the water and a frustrating time. When paddling a canoe tandem, one person should paddle on the left and the other on the right. If both paddlers paddle on the same side it will make the canoe unstable and very difficult to paddle in a straight line. To hold a canoe paddle correctly, one hand should hold onto the T grip with thumb under the grip and fingers over the top. The other hand should be placed between half and two-thirds of the way down the paddle. If you place the paddle horizontally on top of your head, you should form a square: the paddle shaft is the top edge, hand to elbow one side, elbow to neck the bottom edge and neck to head the other side. As your skills progress you will change the grip on your paddle slightly depending on what strokes you are doing and if touring, whitewater paddling or playboating. You may find you are more comfortable with the bottom hand slightly higher up or lower down the paddle shaft.

Holding the paddle correctly is essential to enjoyment and success when canoeing. One paddler should paddle on the right and the other on the left.

Practise all paddling strokes on both sides equally. It is crucial for your development as a canoe paddler that you learn to paddle on both sides. Learning strokes on both sides will take slightly longer, but you will become a better and more balanced canoeist. When paddling tandem you should also swap ends to improve your learning experience.

Teamwork

Teamwork is the key to successful tandem canoe paddling. To work well as a team, tandem canoeists must learn to communicate. If you do not talk through what you are going to do first, the chances of succeeding are vastly reduced and the chances of falling in, or falling out (with each other) are vastly increased. For every movement, whether lifting the canoe from the roof of the car or a change of direction on the water, talk through your plan before proceeding.

Teamwork, trust and communication are three key skills necessary for successful open canoeing. Standing in a canoe is a good test of all three.

Basic skills

There are six basic strokes that every canoeist should learn in order to experience safe and enjoyable days on the water.

The forward stroke

The first and most obvious stroke to learn is the forward paddling stroke; this is the stroke you will use most in your canoeing career and is arguably the most important. A stroke to make to canoe move forwards is easy to work out but a powerful and efficient forward stroke requires practice and thought. To paddle forwards efficiently, reach forward with the paddle and place the whole paddle blade under the water. The reach forward with your whole body should be as far as comfortable without feeling unbalanced or overstretched; for most people this should be about one metre. If you are sitting in the canoe you should feel your weight transferring from your bottom to your heels. If kneeling, you should feel your bottom lifting slightly from the seat and your weight transferring to your knees. Both arms should be extended and your head should remain up, looking where you are going and allowing air to get into your lungs.

The three parts of a good forward paddle stroke: first, reach forward and place the paddle in the water; second, using your whole body pull the paddle through the water; and third, bring the paddle out of the water as it passes your hips. (Note that the paddle blade in this sequence is not completely underwater to show the angle of the paddle blade. During normal paddling the whole paddle blade should be submerged.)

Use your back and shoulders to start to pull the paddle through the water, keeping your arms extended. As the paddle comes through the water push out with your top hand and pull with your lower hand. The forward stroke should finish with the paddle slightly behind your hips with the paddle blade on the surface of the water and your body upright. Recover the paddle to the start of the stroke by twisting the paddle so the blade slices through the air edge first, keeping the blade close above the surface of the water. Replace the paddle in the water and repeat. For tandem canoeing, one paddler should paddle on the left side and the other on the right.

Timing and rhythm is key to efficient tandem canoe paddling. The front paddler should make regular paddling strokes and the back paddler should follow in time. A tandem canoe crew not only paddles better but also looks better if the paddlers keep in time with one another, and we all want to look good when paddling.

The backward stroke

Next on the list of basic strokes to learn is the backward stroke. The action for backwards paddling is similar to paddling forwards except in reverse. You do not need to turn the paddle around to paddle backwards, even if the blade has a curved shape. Keep your hand grip the same and use the back of the paddle blade. Put the paddle blade completely under the water just behind your hips keeping the paddle shaft as vertical as possible. To place the paddle into the water you will have to rotate your torso towards the paddling side. To start the backward stroke, unwind your torso applying the pressure to the paddle blade. As your torso returns to a straight position push out towards the front of the canoe using your bottom hand. As you reach the end of the stroke, pull the T grip back with your top arm.

The most important part of the backward stroke to remember is to look where you are going. Look over your shoulder as you turn your torso to put the paddle into the water. Not only will you be able to see where you are going but, by turning your head in the same direction as your body, you will also improve your torso rotation. Aim to look over your shoulder before every stroke.

When paddling backwards look where you want to go, place the paddle into the water then push it towards the front of the canoe. (Note that the paddle blade in this sequence is not completely underwater to show the angle of the paddle blade. During normal paddling the whole paddle blade should be submerged.)

The recovery is the same as for the forward stroke. Take the paddle blade completely out of the water, twist the paddle ninety degrees and slice it back through the air to the start position. Try to keep the paddle as close to the surface of the water without actually being in the water. As you recover the paddle, turn to look over your shoulder. This will turn your torso and you will be ready to start the next stroke.

Stopping

Knowing where your brakes are is very important, and open canoeing is no exception. There are many occasions when there is a need to slow down or stop, e.g. another canoeist might be in your way or you might be heading towards a rock or the riverbank. When paddling forwards the front paddler will normally be the first to see an obstacle and should call out loudly and clearly "STOP!" Both paddlers should immediately place their paddles in the water at the start position for a backward stroke, just behind the hip. Hold this position until the canoe starts to slow down, and then finish the stroke. Repeat the backward stroke twice after the initial stroke, looking behind you as you put the paddle in the water. After the third stroke the canoe should be travelling backwards in a straight line. Try to keep control of the canoe. If the canoe starts to turn it is probably because one paddler is braking harder than the other.

The emergency stop: hold the paddle in the water to slow down and stop a canoe urgently. Then take two more backward strokes until you are at a standstill or moving slightly backward.

When paddling backwards, braking and stopping is achieved by using forward strokes. Just three strokes should be sufficient to stop the canoe and start it moving in the opposite direction.

Turning the canoe: sweep strokes

The sweep stroke is used to turn the canoe. There are two variants of the sweep stroke: forwards and reverse. When paddling tandem, either stationary or on the move, one paddler should use a forwards sweep and the other a reverse sweep to turn the canoe. When paddling tandem you should only use quarter circle (ninety degrees) sweep strokes. The front paddler sweeps the paddle in a quarter circle from the front of the canoe, while the back paddler sweeps the paddle in a quarter circle from the back of the canoe. Extending the sweep over ninety degrees will not improve the turn and will start to work against the turning motion of the canoe when paddling in tandem.

A tandem pair using 90 degree sweep strokes to turn the canoe on the spot. The front paddler is performing a forwards sweep stroke and the back paddler a reverse sweep stroke.

The sweep stroke is performed by putting the blade into the water at one end of the quarter circle, keeping the paddle as horizontal as possible and the blade as close to the surface of the water as possible during the stroke. Draw out a ninety degree arc in the water with the paddle, take the paddle out of the water and repeat. Try to keep the T grip as stationary as possible during the sweep stoke and to pivot the paddle around it: imagine the paddle is a hand of a clock and the T grip is the centre point. Turn your head to look at the paddle blade during the sweep stroke. This should lead to you turning your torso during the sweep stroke and thus using your body, not just your arms, to move the paddle through the water and turn the canoe.

Steering: stern rudder

This is a stroke that can be used to control the direction of the canoe while on the move without slowing it down. The stern rudder should only be used by the back paddler.

The stern rudder is used to control the direction of a canoe that is moving forwards. By applying pressure to the paddle the direction can be changed.

The paddle blade is placed in the water towards the back of the canoe with the drive face of the paddle towards the canoe. Turn your torso towards the paddle, which assists you in holding the paddle parallel to the canoe, but keep your head facing forwards so you can see where you are going.

The paddle shaft should be held as level as possible. Completely level is generally not possible; the T grip hand above the gunwale and the bottom hand about the height of the gunwale is a good rough guide. Holding the paddle straight will keep a moving canoe travelling in a straight line and can be used to control the canoe when floating with the current on a flowing river. Pushing the paddle blade away from the canoe or pulling the paddle blade towards the canoe will change the direction of the canoe. Pushing the paddle blade away will have a more pronounced turning effect than pulling it towards the canoe. To improve the turning action of pulling the paddle towards the canoe, you can take the paddle out of the water and repeat the stroke.

The key to the stern rudder is to place the paddle blade as far towards the back of the canoe as comfortable. Try not to spend too much time concentrating on the stern rudder. Use it only when necessary. The back paddler should also paddle forwards; it should not be a case of the front paddler doing all the work while the back paddler steers.

Using the draw stroke to move a canoe sideways. Paddlers need to keep in time with each other.

Moving sideways: draw stroke

The next challenge to face is moving the canoe sideways. This is one of the few situations when it is recommended that both paddlers paddle on the same side. Both paddlers should turn their

torso to face the direction in which they wish to move the canoe. Place the paddle vertically in the water with the paddle blade underwater as far away as is comfortable. To move the canoe sideways pull the canoe towards the paddle using mainly your bottom arm; the paddle should remain vertical for the duration of the stroke. Just before the canoe reaches the paddle, slice the blade out of the water behind you by dropping the T grip hand forwards and pivoting the paddle around the bottom hand. Reach out and plant the paddle blade in the water again and repeat. Aim to keep your head up, looking in the direction of travel.

It is possible to use the draw stroke as a turning stroke. If the paddlers use the draw stroke on opposite sides the canoe will turn; this will work when the canoe is stationary or on the move. The draw stroke can be used in combination with a sweep stroke to increase turning efficiency. The paddler in the back performs a forward sweep stroke and the paddler in the front performs a draw stroke. This technique is particularly effective for very tight turns or very quick changes of direction at speed.

When both paddlers perform the draw stroke on the same side, the canoe should move effortlessly sideways. Lift the leading edge of the canoe slightly by pushing your following edge down; this will help the water to travel under the bottom of the canoe.

The capsize drill

At some point in your canoeing career, whether in the first few seconds or much later on, you will capsize. Canoes are generally very stable craft and will not capsize unless severely over balanced. If the canoe does capsize, however, several simple rules apply. Do not panic; you should be wearing a buoyancy aid and it is very unlikely that you will get stuck in the canoe. If you are unable to reach the surface stay calm and try to find the source of your problem. Staying calm will conserve oxygen, allowing you to free yourself from the canoe and swim to the surface. As soon as you

Capsizing is nothing to worry about – in fact, it can be fun. Regular practice will ensure you are confident of your ability to safely capsize and rescue yourself.

are safely floating beside your upturned canoe check to see if your paddling partner is also safe and happy. If your partner is not above the surface your first priority is to find them and try to help them. Stay calm and do not put yourself in unnecessary danger. Try to keep hold of your paddle; you will need it later on in the day. Swim to the end of the canoe and tow it towards the closest dry land. Swimming with the canoe is best done by swimming on your back, holding the canoe at the front with one hand and using the paddle to help you swim with the other. Do not try to climb up onto the upturned canoe or turn it back upright. Both actions will fill the canoe with more water, making it heavier to tow to the side.

After a capsize, swim your canoe to the side and lift it slowly upwards to empty the water out of it.

On a warm sunny day find a safe stretch of water (non-flowing, pollution free and clear of underwater obstructions) and practise capsizing your canoe and rescuing yourself. Test your balance. Try paddling while standing or even balancing on the ends of the boat. If you capsize, you will be able to practise rescuing yourself. It may be worth alerting any onlookers before you start so that nobody thinks you are in any real difficulty and calls for help.

Balancing games such as standing on the gunwales are both fun and good self-rescue practice.

Intermediate skills

Once you have mastered all the basic skills, you should be able to manoeuvre your canoe capably in all directions and capsize confidently. While most of the basic paddle strokes can be satisfactorily performed while sitting, the intermediate strokes are much better performed while kneeling. Many of the intermediate strokes require not only the use of the whole body to perform the paddle stroke but the use of the edges of the canoe. Edging and leaning the canoe is carried out by transferring the weight from one side of the canoe to the other, by lifting one knee and applying pressure with the other.

The photograph on the left shows a paddler performing a stroke on their on-side, left hand on the T grip and the paddle on the right-hand side of the canoe. The photograph on the right shows an off-side stroke being performed, right hand on the T grip and the paddle on the right-hand side of the canoe.

Paddling your canoe on your own, solo paddling, is a skill to master for intermediate canoeists. For solo paddlers, the concept of on-side paddle strokes and off-side paddle strokes comes into play. On-side paddle strokes are normal strokes performed on the paddling side. Off-side strokes are performed by lifting the paddle up over the canoe and placing it in the water on the other side of the canoe to perform a stroke.

A good exercise to practise your balance is to kneel in the canoe, knees as far apart as possible. Hold your paddle above your head and gently rock the canoe from side to side using pressure from your knees, rotating your hips and keeping your spine vertical. It is possible to rock a canoe from gunwale to gunwale, slowly filling it with water.

The Goon stroke and the J stroke

To paddle a canoe solo or to have more control over the direction of the canoe when paddling at the back of a tandem canoe, a stroke that combines a forward stroke and a steering stroke is needed. The Goon stroke is the simplest forward and steering stroke, combining a forward stroke and a stern rudder. Start with a forward paddle stroke and, as the paddle blade reaches your hips, instead of taking the paddle out of the water turn the drive face towards the hull of the canoe and bring the paddle into a stern rudder position. By pushing the paddle away from or pulling the paddle towards the canoe, you can control its direction. When paddling solo this stroke will help to keep the canoe travelling in a straight line. Although simple to explain, it will in reality take a little longer to get the hang of the Goon stroke.

The Goon stroke is an easy way to paddle a canoe forwards when paddling solo. It can be thought of as a forward paddle stroke and stern rudder combo.

THE GOON STROKE IS POPULAR FOR SOLO WHITEWATER CANOES (OC1). MANY EXPERIENCED OC1 PADDLERS CHOOSE TO USE THE GOON STROKE AS THE PRIMARY STROKE. ITS SIMPLICITY ENABLES SWIFT PROGRESS TO BE MADE BY THOSE LEARNING TO PADDLE OC1.

Learn the Goon stroke slowly and gently; too much power on either the forward or turning part of the stroke may cause you to lose control of the canoe, challenging your learning experience. By learning slowly any slight errors can be easily corrected without losing control of the canoe or your patience.

The J stroke also combines a forward paddling stroke and a steering stroke. The J stroke is widely regarded as one of the most important strokes in open canoeing as it is not only key to graceful and efficient solo canoeing, but is also the basis of several advanced canoe strokes.

The J stroke starts with a standard forward paddle stroke. The wrist is then turned down and the power face of the paddle blade is turned away from the canoe.

The easiest way to understand the J stroke is to imagine drawing a J in the water with the paddle (this of course assumes that you paddle on the left-hand side, if you paddle on the right the stroke will look like a Ļ!) Start the stroke at the top of the J and perform a normal forwards paddle stroke. As the paddle reaches the hip turn the drive face of the paddle away from the canoe by turning your T grip hand down, do not adjust your grip on the paddle. To adjust the direction of the canoe, push the paddle blade away from the canoe.

As you turn your T grip hand down to form the steering half of the J stroke turn your torso towards the paddle side, but keep looking ahead at where you are going. Turning your torso will enable you to reach further back with your paddle blade and thus make the turning aspect of the stroke more effective.

Although at first uncomfortable, the J stroke will soon become second nature.

The final point to remember is to learn by paddling at a gentle pace. Applying full power will magnify any errors and it may take you longer to understand the stroke. Once you have mastered the J stroke, you will be able to capably and confidently paddle a canoe either solo or tandem.

The reverse J stroke

The reverse J stroke is combination of a backward stroke and a bow rudder (see below) and is used to steer the canoe when travelling backwards either solo or tandem. When paddling backwards in a tandem canoe, the front paddler should perform the reverse J stroke and the back paddler should use normal backward strokes.

The reverse J stroke is an effective way for a solo paddler to paddle backwards; it is nothing more than a backward stroke and bow rudder combination.

To start the stroke turn your torso, look over your shoulders and place the paddle blade under the water, exactly as you would for a normal backward stroke. As you reach the end of the stroke, turn the paddle ninety degrees so that the drive face of the paddle is towards the canoe. Keep your lower arm extended and bring your top hand with the T grip to your paddle-side shoulder. The paddle should now be in a rudder position and, by pushing away from the canoe with the back of the paddle blade, you can steer the canoe.

Hold the rudder at the end of the stroke for a few extra seconds to ensure that the canoe is travelling backwards in a straight line. If you attach a length of rope to the front of the canoe and let it trail in the water you will be able to see if you are travelling in a straight line. If you keep the rope and the canoe in a straight line, then you are paddling backwards straight.

Stopping

Braking and stopping is slightly trickier when paddling solo. Moving forwards, a combination of two on-side and one off-side backward strokes should be used to stop the canoe. First put the brakes on by holding the paddle by your hip. As the canoe slows, finish the stroke and transfer the paddle across the canoe to the off-side. Make one off-side back stroke using the drive face of the blade and transfer back to the on-side. The last on-side stroke should start the canoe moving backwards; don't forget to look behind you.

The bow rudder and cross bow rudder

The bow and cross bow rudder allow the front paddler in a tandem canoe or a solo canoeist to perform tight turns on the move. They are key strokes to master for whitewater canoeing. The bow rudder is performed on the on-side and the cross bow rudder is performed on the off-side; you should not swap your hand grip

The bow rudder: thumb and T grip on the shoulder, the paddle blade as far forward as comfortable and weight on the inside of the turn.

on the paddle for either stroke. Both strokes are performed using a similar body movement but a slightly different movement with the arms. The paddle position is the same for both the bow and cross bow rudder: blade completely underwater with the drive face parallel to the side of the canoe. The paddle shaft is at an angle of approximately forty-five degrees to the surface of the water and the T grip is level in height with your shoulders.

To perform the bow rudder reach as far forwards as is comfortable towards the front of the canoe with the paddle blade, as if you were about to perform a forward paddle stroke. Turn the drive face of the paddle ninety degrees towards the canoe and place the blade under the water, approximately thirty centimetres from the side of the canoe. The paddle should be at a slight angle, with the back edge of the paddle closer to the canoe than the front edge; if not, make it so. The T grip hand should rest on your shoulder with your thumb touching your collarbone as if going to look at your watch. Your bottom arm should be almost fully extended and tucked into your body to create a strong shape to hold the paddle in the water.

The cross bow rudder: the paddle is lifted over the canoe and placed in the water with the blade towards the front of the canoe.

The cross bow rudder is easier to grasp for many canoeists as the paddle movement is not as complex as the bow rudder. Start by holding the paddle horizontally in front of you at chest height. Rotate your torso so that the paddle has turned ninety degrees and the blade is towards the front of the canoe. Lower your bottom hand until the blade is under the water; the blade should be about thirty centimetres from the canoe. Twist the paddle with the T grip hand so the bottom edge of the paddle is slightly closer to the canoe than the top edge. The paddle shaft should be at an angle of around forty-five degrees, your bottom arm almost fully extended and your top arm bent at the elbow. Try not to squash your body; keep your head up and maintain a good posture.

Turning your head and leaning the canoe into the turn will increase the effectiveness of both a bow and a cross bow rudder.

There are two ways to improve the bow and cross bow rudder. Turn your head to look in the direction you intend to turn. Not only can you now see where you are going but it also helps to rotate your torso in that direction, improving the dynamics of the stroke. Lean the canoe into the turn as much as you dare. The faster you are travelling, the easier it is to lean in (imagine a skier or mountain biker making a fast turn). Pick up some forward speed then lift your paddle out of the water. Turn your head and lean the canoe in the same direction by pressing down with your knee on that side. The canoe will turn in a wide arc without the need for paddle strokes. Now combine this action with a bow or cross bow rudder and – hey, presto! – you have a super-efficient tight turning stroke.

Leaning the canoe into the turn will help to turn the canoe even without the use of the paddle.

The bow draw and cross bow draw

A continuation from the bow and cross bow rudder is to follow them with a draw stroke element. Start the stroke with the paddle further away from the canoe than a bow rudder. Turn your head and lean into the turn. As the canoe starts to turn, pull the paddle through the water towards the front of the canoe. The whole stroke should follow a quarter circle in the water, with the paddle finishing up with the blade almost touching the front of the canoe. You can repeat this stroke several times to perform a tight and controlled turning manoeuvre on either flat water or whitewater.

A bow draw is a combination of a bow rudder and a draw stroke: start with the paddle much further away and draw it towards the front of the canoe.

A cross bow draw is exactly the same combination of a cross bow rudder and a draw stroke. Lift the paddle over the canoe as if to perform a cross bow rudder, but reach a little bit further before placing the paddle into the water. Once in the water, draw the paddle towards the front of the canoe in a quarter circle arc and lift it out just before it reaches the canoe.

A cross bow draw.

The inside pivot turn

The inside pivot turn will not work in a tandem canoe. To start the turn, place the paddle in the water behind you and perform a ninety degree backward sweep stroke. When the paddle reaches the end of the sweep, twist the whole paddle 180 degrees so the drive face of the paddle is facing forwards. Hold the T grip on your shoulder as you would when performing a bow rudder. Draw the paddle towards the front of the canoe. Recover the paddle back to the start of the stroke by slicing it back through the water towards the back of the canoe. The paddle is now back at the start position and you can repeat the stroke.

The inside pivot turn is a very elegant way to turn a canoe on the spot. It can be used on flat water, on whitewater and for flat water freestyle. It is basically a back sweep stroke for 90 degrees, turn the paddle 180 degrees towards you, then a bow draw.

When recovering the paddle back through the water, be careful to keep a little space between the paddle and the canoe. If the paddle blade goes too far under the canoe, it can lead to a very unstable moment and possibly loss of the paddle (or worse, a capsize). If you find the paddle is under the canoe and making you unstable, the best solution is to let go of the paddle with the T grip hand. If you then lean forwards, keeping hold of the paddle with the bottom hand, the paddle will float out from under the canoe and you can start again.

With practice, this stroke can be performed effortlessly and smoothly and will turn the canoe very gracefully on the spot. It is also very useful for slowing the canoe to turn into tight eddies on whitewater, and is one of the key strokes to learn for flat water freestyle canoeing.

Outside pivot turn

The outside pivot turn is a combination of a forward sweep stroke and a cross bow draw. You can start an outside pivot turn with either a forward sweep or a cross bow draw, although the turn will work better when finished with a sweep stroke. Kneeling is the best position to adopt for the pivot turn, as it enables you to rotate your torso effectively. Keep the paddle as horizontal as possible and maintain a good balanced position in the canoe.

The outside pivot turn is a combination between a cross bow draw and a forward sweep stroke. This linked stroke is particularly useful for breaking into eddies on whitewater.

To start an outside pivot turn with a cross bow draw, reach over the gunwales and place the paddle into the water. Adjust the angle of the hull if necessary, and draw the paddle towards the canoe.

As the blade reaches the canoe lift it up out of the water and back over the gunwales and into the water at the start position for a forward sweep stroke. Follow the blade with your head during the whole stroke. Turning your head during the stroke will start your torso rotating, improving the reach and efficiency of the stroke.

Starting the outside pivot turn with a cross bow draw enables you to perform a tighter turn than if you start with a sweep stroke. Starting with a forward sweep stroke is a popular choice for paddlers wishing to turn into eddies on moving water.

As you turn your torso during the turn, allow the canoe to slip slightly under your knees. By changing your position slightly in the canoe you will increase your reach and angle of the stroke. One of the great advantages of the canoe is that you can move around in the boat; take advantage of this whenever possible.

Feathered draw

From the draw (moving sideways) stroke you can progress to the feathered draw. The feathered draw looks more elegant, but the standard draw stroke is quicker and more powerful. Start as for a draw stroke i.e. torso turned to the direction of travel, both arms extended out and paddle vertical with the blade under the water. Start by pulling the canoe towards the paddle. Just before the canoe reaches the paddle, twist the paddle ninety degrees (either direction will work) and slice the paddle back away from the canoe. To start the next feathered draw stroke, twist the paddle blade back so it is parallel to the canoe.

When performing any type of draw stroke, you should lift the leading edge of the canoe slightly. By lifting the edge of the canoe you will help it to glide efficiently over the water. If you lean the canoe towards the paddle when draw stroking, you will dig the leading edge into the water. This will cause resistance and make the stroke less efficient.

The feathered draw starts as a normal draw stroke. When the paddle reaches the canoe, turn it 90 degrees and slice it away from the canoe back to the start point of the stroke; then repeat the draw stroke.

The feathered draw can also be performed as an off-side stroke. Simply lift the paddle up and over the gunwales, turn your torso and place the paddle into the water on the off-side. Perform the off-side feathered draw using exactly the same action as for a feathered draw. Be aware that you will need to twist the paddle and slice it forwards slightly earlier when it is on the off-side, to reduce the chance of catching the blade under the hull of the canoe and potentially capsizing.

Sculling draw

The sculling draw is one of the most rewarding canoe strokes to learn and master. It allows the paddler to perform an everlasting draw stroke and change the angle of the canoe, at the same time if necessary. To start the sculling draw, turn your head and torso ninety degrees so you are facing sideways. Move your knees around if this helps to increase your torso rotation. Place the paddle blade under the water, approximately thirty-five centimetres from the side of the canoe. Twist the angle of the paddle blade so that the front-facing edge is slightly further away from the canoe than the following edge of the paddle. Imagine drawing a figure-of-eight in the water with the paddle, starting at the bottom left-hand corner. Aim to slice the paddle to the top right corner of the figure-of-eight while simultaneously applying a pulling pressure on the paddle blade. When the paddle arrives at the top right corner, change the angle of the blade and slice it back towards the top left corner of the figure-of-eight while pulling on the paddle to draw the canoe sideways.

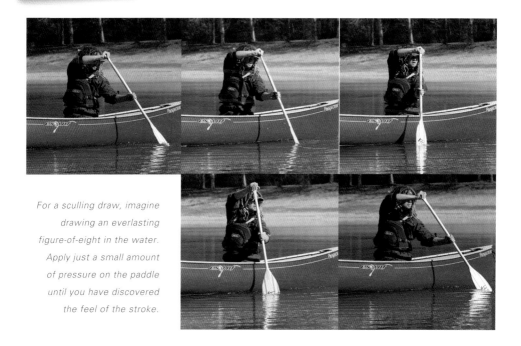

For a sculling draw, imagine drawing an everlasting figure-of-eight in the water. Apply just a small amount of pressure on the paddle until you have discovered the feel of the stroke.

As with most paddle strokes, the sculling draw should be performed slowly whilst you learn. Subtle changes in the angle of the paddle and the application of only a small amount of power will move the canoe effortlessly sideways. The key to learning is to experiment; learn which angles work most efficiently and when is it best to apply full power during the stroke.

Pry

The pry stroke is the exact opposite of the draw stroke. Instead of pulling the canoe towards the paddle, the paddle is used to move the canoe away. The action for a pry stroke is similar to the action of a feathered draw, but in reverse.

To pry the canoe away from the paddle, place the blade into the water next to the canoe. Hook your bottom hand over the gunwale and lever the paddle away from the canoe.

Start the pry stroke with the paddle blade under the water and the shaft vertical against the side of the canoe. Turn your head and torso to face the paddle as you would if performing a draw stroke. Hold the paddle against the side of the canoe by clamping your fingers to the outside of the gunwale and thumb to the inside of the gunwale. Lever the paddle away from the canoe by pulling the T grip hand towards your shoulder. As with the draw stroke, remember to lift the leading edge of the canoe by applying pressure with your knees. When you feel you are no longer pushing the canoe sideways but instead digging the canoe into the water, twist the paddle ninety degrees and slice it back through the water to the start position and repeat.

By placing the paddle blade deep in the water, a very pronounced sideways movement can be achieved with only a very subtle hand movement. If you are pry stroking on moving water, be careful not to catch the blade on a rock under the water. Maintain a light grip with the T grip hand so that the paddle can be released quickly if necessary.

Low brace

Having learnt to capsize your canoe safely, the next skill is to learn how to prevent accidental capsize. The easiest stroke to learn to prevent your canoe from capsizing is the low brace. The low brace is performed by holding the paddle horizontal, parallel to the surface of the water with the T grip over the middle of the canoe. Lean forwards to transfer your weight onto your knees and hold the paddle so that your upper body is above the paddle. This will help you to gain maximum support from the paddle.

The low brace: keep your arms and shoulders over the paddle shaft and push down and forwards on the paddle blade. Aim to keep the blade on the surface of the water.

As the canoe starts to tip and become unstable, reach out with the paddle in the low brace position. As the canoe tips, push down on the surface of the water with the paddle blade. Use the resistance of the water to support the weight of your body and slow down the tipping motion of the canoe. To recover the canoe into a stable position, keep your weight over the paddle and tip the canoe back to a stable position by applying pressure to the canoe through your knees, transferring your weight back from the paddle to your knees. It will sometimes be necessary to brace several times to be sure of stabilising the canoe and preventing a capsize.

Lean forwards when low bracing. Leaning forwards lowers your centre of gravity and increases the weight you can transfer onto the paddle. As you push your weight down onto the paddle, roll your wrists forwards. This action will help keep the paddle blade near the surface of the water. The deeper the paddle goes, the less effective the brace.

Advanced skills

The strokes covered in this section are by no means a complete collection of all advanced strokes and techniques. They are merely a collection of some of the most useful and interesting skills that an advanced open canoeist may need. An advanced open canoeist should be aware of how to use the edge of the canoe and be comfortable with leaning the canoe so that the gunwale touches the water. Several of these strokes require the use a touring canoe paddle to perform them at their best. Many of the strokes at the advanced level should be experimented with in order to find the best solution for each paddler, canoe and situation. Try to learn something new every time you visit the river. Good luck!

Knifed J and Canadian stroke

At the end of your J stroke, knife the paddle back through the water. Try not to put pressure on the blade but just slice it through the water.

These are two very similar strokes that are subtly different. If the paddle blade is used actively during the recovery phase of the stroke to control the direction of the canoe, the stroke is a Canadian stroke. If the blade is not actively used during the recovery phase of the stroke, it is a knifed J.

The paddle movement for a **knifed J** is very similar to that of a J stroke; it is just the recovery at the end of the stroke that is slightly different. The knifed J is a natural progression from the J stroke and many canoeists will have unknowingly adapted their J stroke to a knifed J. Once a J stroke has been completed, instead of taking the paddle blade out of the water and recovering it to the start of stroke, keep the blade in the water. Recover the paddle blade to the start of the stroke simply by slicing it back through the water. The advantage of keeping the blade underwater means it can be used to control the direction of the canoe should an unexpected gust of wind affect the direction of travel.

The **Canadian stroke** starts with a forward paddle stroke. As the paddle reaches your hip, turn your T grip hand thumb down as you would for a J stroke. Instead of turning the thumb all the way down, turn it only forty-five degrees so that the drive face of the paddle is facing upwards. Keeping pressure on the paddle blade, lift it forwards through the water until it reaches the surface. This pressure on the paddle enables you to control the direction of the canoe. The slicing movement is similar to that of a quarter sweep stroke; it starts at the back of the canoe and should finish level with the hip.

The movement of the Canadian stroke is almost identical to the knifed J. The difference is the amount of pressure applied to the paddle, which should be lifted as it is sliced through the water.

As you slice the paddle forwards through the water, aim to keep the paddle away from the gunwale. Prying off or dragging the paddle along the gunwale not only creates noise but also unnecessary wear and tear on both gunwales and paddles.

Kneeling provides a distinct advantage for performing both the knifed J and Canadian strokes. Kneel with knees together and to-

PRYING THE PADDLE OFF THE GUNWALE IS KNOWN AS 'CLONKING' BECAUSE OF THE NOISE IT MAKES.

wards the paddling side; turn your body slightly towards the paddle. The uneven nature of this sitting position – ideal for calm touring paddling – is unsuitable for whitewater or windy conditions.

Indian stroke

The Indian stroke also originated in North America, first developed by Native Americans as a stroke to use while hunting from an open canoe. Done well, this stroke can move the canoe silently through the water. A modern-day application of this stroke is to use it when approaching wildlife to avoid scaring the animal or bird before you are within camera range. The Indian stroke is also very useful for keeping control of a canoe on very windy sections of water as the paddle blade remains constantly in the water and ensures you have constant control over your canoe.

The Indian stroke allows the paddle and the canoe to move silently over the water. Note how little disturbance there is as the paddle slices forwards through the water.

The basic principles of the Indian stroke are simple. The start of the stroke is the same as any other forward canoe stroke: steer by pushing the blade out, similar to the knifed J stroke. Slice the blade back towards the front of the canoe without taking the blade out of the water for the start of the next stroke.

The key concept for the Indian stroke is to use alternate sides of the paddle blade for each stroke, rotating the T grip in the open palm of your hand during each stroke. Imagine the paddle travelling around in an oval shape in the water.

C stroke

The C stroke is a combination of a bow draw and a J stroke. It acquired its name from the movement of the paddle through the water in the shape of a C (when performed on the right-hand side of the canoe). The C stroke is particularly useful for paddling into a head wind and for paddling OC1 whitewater canoes. To start, place the paddle into the water at the front of the canoe and perform a shortened bow draw. The bow draw should be just enough to turn the front of the canoe slightly towards the paddle side. As the paddle nears the side of the canoe, twist the paddle so it is in the position to start a J stroke and continue through with the stroke to the finish. You should find you need to steer slightly less than with the J stroke as you have already turned the canoe with the bow draw at the start of the stroke.

The C stroke is a proactive steering stroke. Start with a bow draw then follow straight into a standard J stroke.

The C stroke allows the paddler to steer the bow of the canoe before the power phase of the stroke. The forward stroke corrects the direction of the canoe instead of pushing it off course (which would require a corrective rudder stroke at the end) so the C stroke is a proactive (as opposed to reactive) steering stroke.

Bow jam and cross bow jam

These strokes will turn the canoe very sharply when performed by a solo canoeist or the front paddler in a tandem canoe. The jam is best described as the opposite to a bow rudder; instead of turning towards the paddle as in a bow rudder, the bow jam will turn the canoe away from the paddle. During your paddling career you will have learnt that when the paddle blade catches or jams under the canoe it will unbalance the canoe and turn it around. The bow jam harnesses this reaction and turns it into a very powerful paddle stroke.

The bow jam is a tricky stroke to learn. The secret is to hold the paddle firmly to prevent it going under the canoe.

For a bow jam the canoe must be moving; starting slow until you become more confident, when you can pick up the pace. Reach forwards with the paddle in a position similar to a bow rudder. Place the paddle into the water with the drive face pushed against the side of the canoe and the following edge turned furthest away from the hull. As soon as the paddle is placed in this position it will feel as if it is about to be ripped out of your hands (if not, you will surely follow it under the canoe). For the bow jam to be a success, good balance and active edge control is needed. Edge the canoe to the paddle side, hang on to the paddle and turn your head to look in the direction you wish to turn, not at the paddle. It can be very easy to capsize when practising and performing the bow jam, and it is better to release the paddle than capsize.

In a tandem, the back paddler can assist by initiating the turn with a short backward sweep stroke and then standing by with a low brace in case of a loss of balance. A solo paddler can start the turn, do the jam stroke and balance the canoe all on their own.

As with the bow jam, hold the paddle firmly in place and control the balance of the canoe through your knees.

The cross bow jam follows all the same principles as the bow jam. The paddle is held in the same position as a cross bow rudder but with the paddle blade turned towards the canoe and held against the hull. I find the cross bow jam easier to perform solo than a bow jam and it is also easier to perform tandem because the back paddler is able to low brace to prevent a capsize.

As with all new strokes, learn the bow jams slowly. If you accelerate to full speed then jam the paddle against the side of the canoe for your first attempt you will almost certainly capsize, much to the amusement of any onlookers. Experiment with the placement of the paddle and the angle of the blade initially at a slow speed, gradually building up your confidence.

Hanging draw and hanging pry

The hanging draw is one of the most challenging open canoe strokes to master. However, remembering to look where you are going and lifting the leading edge of the canoe makes the stroke much more achievable. The hanging draw and hanging pry are both strokes that will only work when the canoe is moving. Both can be very useful for side slipping the canoe when navigating technical rapids.

Once mastered, the hanging draw produces a pronounced sideways movement by using the forward momentum of the canoe.

Place the paddle blade in the water in a similar position to the start of a draw stroke. With the blade underwater and the paddle shaft vertical, twist your torso in the direction of the paddle but keep your head looking forwards in the direction of travel. For the hanging draw, cock your wrists so the forward edge of the paddle blade is further away from the canoe than the following edge so that it can slice forwards and sideways. Apply a slight pulling pressure. This gentle pulling combined with the forward motion should make the canoe glide forwards and sideways simultaneously.

If the canoe starts to turn instead of moving sideways, this is probably because the paddle has been placed too far forwards and is acting like a bow rudder instead of a draw stroke. The solution is move the paddle further back in the water.

A hanging pry is very similar to a hanging draw, except that the leading edge of the paddle blade should be set so that it is closer to the canoe than the following edge. When moving at a reasonable speed, twist your torso and place the paddle under the water. Apply a slight pushing pressure to the back of the blade and lift the leading edge of the canoe. The canoe should start to move sideways away from the paddle.

The hanging pry moves the canoe sideways. First build up the speed, lift the leading edge of the canoe and place the paddle blade in the water with the blade angled towards the front of the canoe.

Do not expect to master these strokes first time. Experiment with the position of the paddle in the water until it works for you. Each canoe, paddler and seating position requires a slightly different placement of the paddle in the water. Once mastered, the hanging draw and hanging pry are two of the most useful moving water strokes at your disposal.

Off-side brace

One of the most challenging situations for the solo canoeist is to prevent the canoe from capsizing when it tips away from the on-side. With no paddle blade on the off-side to provide support, frantically waving the T grip in the air will not prevent a deter-mined canoe from capsizing. Swapping the paddle over at the last second is not a feasible option either. Thankfully, there is a simple solution (two in fact): a draw or pry stroke. Both work for the same reasons and are equally as effective.

Preventing an open canoe from capsizing on the non-paddle side: a draw stroke or a pry can be used to help recover the balance of the canoe as it tips away from the paddle.

As the canoe starts to capsize away from the paddle you should quickly transfer your weight across to the higher edge of the canoe. By performing a draw or a pry stroke you will be able to gain some stability from the paddle as it grips under the water, allowing you to literally pull the canoe back from the brink of capsize. The pry support stroke tends to work better in smaller whitewater canoes while the draw support works better in larger traditional canoes.

This off-side brace relies more on good edge control and balance than on the actual stroke used. The draw or pry stroke will help to keep the canoe under control as you re-balance the canoe.

New paddle strokes

Every stroke described here and many others exist only because of the curiosity of canoeists and their eagerness to explore and invent. Use every trip to the river as an opportunity to learn and explore new ways to move your paddle through the water and therefore your canoe across the water. Don't get hung up on the names of each stroke; there are far too many to remember. Simply aim to discover how to move your canoe efficiently across the water.

WHITEWATER

The challenge of paddling rapids fascinates many canoeists.

Descending rapids is a challenge that canoeists have taken on since the pioneers of paddlesports first rode rapids sitting astride their log canoes. Safely descending the rapid was the goal and rapids were an inconvenience rather than a playground. For modern recreational canoeists, moving water and rapids provide a challenging environment in which to learn and practise skills. This chapter will explore the skills necessary to paddle your canoe safely and successfully on moving water and rapids.

River grading and guidebooks

THE INFORMATION CONTAINED IN GUIDEBOOKS CAN ONLY BE GUARANTEED AS ACCURATE AT THE TIME THE RIVER WAS PADDLED BY THE AUTHOR. A GUIDE IS JUST THAT: ONE PERSON'S OPINION OF A RIVER.

Rapids are grouped into six classes or grades. This system is recognised worldwide but is very much open to interpretation. The system was devised so that competent paddlers can make an educated decision about whether a river is suitable and safe to attempt. A guidebook will suggest put-in and take-out points, any known hazards to be aware of, the distance and approximate time needed, the most suitable time of year to paddle the river and a grading of the river.

Try to gain as much local knowledge as possible about the area you intend to explore by contacting local clubs or individuals to gain up-to-date information on the condition of the river. Rivers of all grades can pose a danger to an unprepared or inexperienced canoeist. Make sensible and safe decisions and you will enjoy canoeing; make reckless decisions and you risk misadventure.

Grade one and grade two whitewater.

Grade one rapids feature slow moving water possibly with a few waves and ripples. Successful navigation down the river should be achievable to all paddlers with a basic skill level.

Grade two rapids feature more continuous and faster flowing water with more frequent waves, hazards and irregular currents. Navigation is possible for skilled paddlers as a clear line down the rapid is easily identifiable and achievable.

Grade three and grade four whitewater.

Grade three rapids feature medium sized waves, irregular currents from multiple directions and small hazards in the line of navigation. Experienced paddlers should be able to identify a safe line from above the rapid without having to climb out of their canoe to inspect. Descending a grade three rapid is possible for experienced moving-water paddlers, but a mistake could lead to injury or damage to equipment. Grade three whitewater is considered the limit for traditional open canoes on whitewater by most paddlers.

Grade four rapids are identified by long complex rapids with large waves, multiple hazards and an obvious gradient; they provide a good challenge for expert paddlers. The line through the rapid may not be obvious at first glance and may require inspection from the river bank. The rapids pose a significant danger to the inexperienced or inappropriately equipped paddler. Paddlers wishing to attempt grade four whitewater and above should use specifically designed and outfitted whitewater canoes.

Grade five rapids are a serious undertaking for expert canoeists. Long technical rapids featuring many hazards and multiple drops confront the paddler. The complex nature of the rapid makes the line unclear to the inexperienced paddler and bank side inspection vital to any prospective paddlers. A mistake at this level will lead to a very uncomfortable situation, damage to and possible loss of equipment and a physically demanding swim for the paddler.

Grade five and grade six whitewater.

Grade six rapids are the very limit of navigation, only possible by expert canoeists at ideal water levels. Intimidating rapids, steep drops, constant gradient and chaotic currents challenge the paddler. A mistake could prove fatal.

Medical emergencies

YOU MAY BE ABLE TO MAKE EMERGENCY PHONE CALLS FROM YOUR MOBILE EVEN IF YOU DO NOT HAVE NETWORK COVERAGE. MOST PHONES WILL ALLOW YOU TO DIAL EMERGENCY SERVICES ON ANY AVAILABLE NETWORK.

All paddlers who travel to areas that are not immediately accessible to the emergency services should learn and practise CPR (cardiopulmonary resuscitation) and first aid. Some basic medical knowledge can prevent minor injuries turning into emergencies. For day trips on your local river, a basic first aid kit will suffice. For multi-day wilderness trips a comprehensive medical kit should be packed and several members of the group trained to use its contents. You may be hours or even days from the nearest doctor or hospital. A mobile or satellite phone and a list of local emergency numbers will enable professional help to be summoned if coverage allows; 112 can be used to contact the emergency services worldwide.

Safety equipment for moving water

The very nature of moving water and rapids presents risks and hazards to paddlers. To enjoy a safe experience on the river we should do everything possible to reduce the risks and avoid the hazards. Choose a river to paddle appropriate to your ability level. Carry suitable safety equipment and know how to use it and, if an incident occurs, deal with it capably and calmly.

In order to enjoy a day on moving water some basic safety equipment is required. A correctly fitting helmet and buoyancy aid and a solid pair of shoes are basic requirements, along with appropriate clothing for the weather conditions and water temperature.

Throw bag

A throw bag is a rescue device designed to allow a rescuer to easily throw a rope to the victim. Fifteen to twenty metres of floating rope are contained within a buoyant and hardwearing fabric bag.

Throw bags should adhere to the 'clean line' principle. This means that the end of the rope not attached to the bag is free from knots. A rope without knots is less likely to be snagged or trapped. Carrying your throw bag on a belt system around your waist guarantees that it is always to hand if needed in an emergency.

A throw bag: carry one around your waist so it is always ready. On the left is a 15 metre personal throw bag. On the right is a rescue bag containing static, non-stretch rope for setting up rope systems to rescue canoes or people.

Rescue knife

Every canoeist who carries a throw bag should also carry a sharp knife in case the need arises to cut themselves or a fellow paddler free from tangled rope. A fixed blade or locking blade knife is suitable for canoeing; a multi-tool knife is not.

A sharp knife that you can use one-handed is an essential tool for all paddlers who value their safety and that of their friends on the river.

When canoeing, you should keep your rescue knife in a place that is quickly accessible. Storing it at the bottom of your dry bag is no good: in a buoyancy aid front pocket or mounted on the buoyancy aid is ideal. You should be able to access your knife with one hand. If it has a folding blade ensure that you can open it using just one hand. A rubberised handle will help you to keep hold of the knife when it is wet or you have cold hands.

Some paddlers tie their knife to their buoyancy aid with a length of cord. The advantage is that if you drop the knife you can retrieve it; the disadvantage is you could be tumbled around underwater attached to a sharp knife. I prefer not to tie my knife to my buoyancy aid and trust my grip.

Rescue equipment

Many paddlers who have attended a swiftwater rescue course carry a collection of items to assist them when setting up rescue

Whistles are good for communicating over long distances and attracting attention. Carry one within easy reach on your buoyancy aid.

and recovery systems. A basic rescue kit will consist of a throw bag, a four metre long tape sling, two prussic loops and two screwgate HMS style karabiners. A tape sling is more versatile than a sewn sling and screwgate karabiners are less likely to accidentally open than snapgates.

A few simple items will help in many river recovery problems: a rescue line, karabiners, prussic loops, a tape sling and pulleys.

Paddlers should also carry a second throw bag, several extra screwgate karabiners and two pulleys. Whenever venturing out onto the river, a suitable first aid kit for both yourself and your canoe should be carried. A roll of gaffer tape provides a good solution to many first aid and repair problems.

Equipping your canoe

It is not only the paddlers who need extra equipment to tackle moving water; your canoe will need some extra outfitting to make it suitable for moving water. First and most important is extra flotation: you will need to fit airbags to your canoe. Airbags will help to displace water in the event of a capsize and make rescuing and recovering the canoe much easier. Airbags should be securely fixed to the canoe using deck lashing and anchor straps and kept fully inflated when paddling.

Canoes designed specifically for whitewater often feature extra internal fittings such as a foam saddle, hip pads and thigh or lap straps. These fittings are designed to hold the paddler in place and improve the handling of the canoe in moving water.

(Left) a saddle and quick release thigh straps for whitewater. (Right) well fitted with airbags.

You should fit comfortably into your chosen craft and be able to quickly and easily exit your canoe both above and below water in case of an emergency. If you chose to use a strap system, ensure that it is fitted with quick release buckles and that you are able to release them quickly and with ease. A strap system without a quick release mechanism should never be used. You should also be able to exit the canoe without releasing the straps.

Both these canoes are suitable for tandem use on whitewater, the bottom canoe has been specially design and outfitted for whitewater paddling and the canoe above is an expedition canoe that has been retro outfitted for whitewater.

On moving water a spare paddle should always be carried. Losing or breaking a paddle should be avoided but, if it does occur, should not cause a problem. A spare paddle should be carried so that it is secured to the canoe but easily accessible when needed.

Features found on moving water

⚠️ **IF THE ANSWER TO ANY OF THESE QUESTIONS IS NO, YOU MUST REALISE THAT RUNNING THE RAPID IS A POTENTIALLY DANGEROUS DECISION. THIS IS THE MOST BASIC FORM OF RIVER GRADING: EITHER THE RAPID IS ACHIEVABLE OR NOT.**

CAN I SEE AN ACHIEVABLE LINE?

DO I EXPECT A POSITIVE OUTCOME IF I DECIDE TO RUN THE RAPID?

CAN ADEQUATE SAFETY COVER BE PUT IN PLACE TO RESCUE ME IN CASE OF A SWIM?

Moving water is very powerful and must be respected. Do not try to work against the force of the river; use it to help you on your way. Don't be scared by the river and its features, enjoy yourself when paddling. Scared and stressed paddlers do not perform at their best and are more likely to make mistakes. Build up your experience and understanding on easier rivers and progress onto harder water when you are good and ready.

Identifying the features on the river will help you to choose a safe route down a rapid. The river's flow is affected by the shape of the river bed, the shape of the river bank and any physical obstructions. The key is learning to identify these features and planning your route down the river accordingly, avoiding any obstacles that may cause you difficulty or danger.

Eddies

Where the flow is obstructed by a protrusion on the river bank, a rock or a bridge stanchion, an area of slow moving or slack water is formed on the downstream side of the obstruction known as an **eddy**. Here you can stop and rest, inspect the next rapid or climb in and out of the canoe. Between the eddy and the main flow there will be an **eddy line**. This narrow band of turbulent water marks the boundary between the main current and the eddy.

An eddy is formed on the downstream side of an obstruction in moving water. Most eddies are safe for canoeists and provide a good opportunity to stop, rest and plan your next move.

V shapes in the river

Downstream Vs are an indication of a route that is most likely to be free from obstructions. When the river is squeezed through a tight gap the water is squashed together as it flows downstream, the result is the shape of a V. Paddling directly into the V and over the point is normally the easiest line that can be run as the water is at its deepest and least turbulent.

A downstream V shape formed as the water flows between two rocks; here the canoeist is crossing from one side of the V to the other.

Upstream Vs are formed when the water flows around an obstruction, such as a rock, which is just under the water, the point of the V points to the obstruction. Paddlers should avoid the middle point of an upstream V but can use the sides of the upstream V to pick up extra speed. Eddies are often formed behind the point of upstream Vs.

Waves

One of the defining features of moving water is standing waves. They vary in size and power but are all formed in a similar way. When moving water flows over an underwater obstruction, the water is forced up and over it. Depending on the shape of the obstruction, the wave may be shallow faced and smooth, or steep faced with a frothy foam pile on top.

Waves are often found one after another decreasing in size as they progress downstream. Such a collection of waves is known as a **wave train**.

Stoppers

Stoppers are found on every whitewater river; some stoppers are friendly, others are dangerous. A stopper is formed by re-circulating water and can have the power to stop the progress of a canoe. The most dangerous stoppers can also re-circulate swimmers. If you are unable to identify the stopper as safe you should consider it dangerous and avoid it. If a stopper is noisy and features a lively foam pile it is safe to assume most of the energy is being dissipated on the surface and therefore the stopper is likely to be friendly. A quiet stopper with little or no surface disturbance will be dissipating its energy underwater; this stopper will probably be unfriendly and should be avoided. Stoppers with no exit points should also be avoided for obvious reasons – if you cannot see a way out you should not go in.

Surfing a stopper. It is safe to play in this small stopper and practise exit strategies.

Skills for moving water

A calculated descent of a rapid or river is much more than simply floating downstream. Attaining tricky eddies and surfing river waves are just two of the many rewards available to skilful whitewater paddlers. There are a few other things you should practise.

The thrill of the rapids.

Swimming

Flowing water is very powerful and most people will struggle to stand still in water greater than knee depth. The pressure of the water forces you downstream; you are no longer in complete control and are, to a certain extent, at the mercy of the river.

Trying to stand up in moving water and rapids is one of the most dangerous situations we can put ourselves in. The uneven nature of the river bed can easily trap the foot of an unsuspecting canoeist between two rocks. The force of the water on your legs pushes you over and underwater. If the water is greater than knee depth you will not be able to support your head above the water to breathe. This situation is known as a 'foot entrapment' – rescue must come very quickly. The rescue team has just a few minutes from when the victim goes under to support their head above water, set up a rescue system and extract them. In many places rescue may be impossible! If you find yourself losing your footing, stop trying to wade and swim. To reduce the likelihood of putting yourself and your paddling buddies through a very stressful rescue situation, adopt one of two whitewater swimming styles.

Defensive swimming: to safely swim in whitewater, lie on your back with your feet in front of you and your arms outstretched.

The **defensive swimming** position is the default: if in doubt swim defensively. Lie back in the water (your buoyancy aid will help you float) with your feet pointing downstream, legs slightly bent and your arms extended out to the sides. Keep your feet on the surface of the water with your toes out of the water. This will greatly reduce the chance of a foot entrapment and will allow you to fend off any oncoming rocks with your feet. Keeping your arms extended in the water will allow you to manoeuvre in the rapid, provide a clear target for a throw bag rescue and keep your body and head stable in rough water. Relax to conserve energy, look towards your potential rescuers and listen out for instructions.

Aggressive swimming: keep your head up out of the water and swim in a straight line to your goal.

Aggressive swimming should be used to move quickly in short bursts towards a point of safety. It is possible to swim aggressively in any swimming style. If the water is deep you can swim on your front; if it is shallow stay on your back. Try to keep your head out of the water to receive instructions and encouragement from your rescuers and look where you are going. In fast flowing water, the quickest way to get to the side is to swim at ninety degrees to the current as powerfully as possible. Continue swimming until you feel the riverbed pushing on the front of your buoyancy aid and then crawl out of the river!

⚠️ A capsized canoe will move at the same speed as the river. If it is full of water, it can weigh as much as a small family car. Avoid being in a position with the canoe upstream of you, as it may squash you on a rock. Swim to the upstream end of the canoe and turn it the right way up, making it easier to swim to the side. Hold on to the end grab with one hand and swim for the side (you may choose to put your paddle back into the canoe).

NO SIGNAL, NO GO

IF YOU DO NOT SEE OR UNDERSTAND A SIGNAL STAY PUT AND WAIT UNTIL YOU RECEIVE A CLEAR AND UNDERSTANDABLE SIGNAL.

Communication: river signals

Paddlers have devised a system of signals to communicate the most common messages. The noise made by rapids can interfere with verbal communication and increase the risk of being misunderstood. Agree which signals mean what with your paddling buddies before getting on the water; this is especially important if you are paddling with a group for the first time.

You

Come to me

Stop

If you only want to communicate a signal to one person, point at them first.

A beckoning motion with one arm is a signal used to communicate to other paddlers that they should come towards you.

A hand held up with the palm towards you means stop. If you do not see a signal when you are expecting one you should also stop and wait.

Go that way

An arm or paddle pointing means paddle in that direction. Always indicate the direction of travel, not the direction of obstacles or dangers. Rapid repetition of the direction may mean you will need to work hard to get the indicated line.

Break out

A horizontally circling hand is a signal that means break out into the next safe eddy. It is usually followed by a direction signal to indicate the direction of the eddy.

OK

Are you OK? I'm OK. Placing a fist on your head or helmet can be used as both a question and answer to check whether everybody is happy and comfortable on the river or to confirm that the signal has been understood.

Let's go

A clenched fist above a vertical forearm moving vertically up and down means let's go. Imagine the action of a steam train driver pulling the whistle chain, "whoop whoop!"

Obstruction

Forearms crossed above the head indicates a serious obstacle in the river. All paddlers should breakout into the nearest eddy and not advance any further. A portage is likely.

Get out and inspect

Pointing towards your eyes with your first and index fingers indicates that it is necessary to climb out of the canoe and inspect the next rapid or drop.

For river signals to be an effective form of communication, a line of sight needs to be established and maintained. Line of sight means keeping the group together so that each paddler can see at least one person in front and at least one person behind them.

Rescue: throw bagging

A throw bag is a tool that can be used to rescue a person from the river. The key to success is regular practice.

Choosing a safe and stable place to stand is key to a good throw bag rescue.

Before throwing a throw bag, first choose a place to stand where you have a good footing and grip; the last thing you want is to be pulled into the river by your victim. Hold the throw bag by the neck with your throwing hand, take out and coil a few metres of rope and hold it in your non-throwing hand. Aim to throw the rope over the victim and across their body so it is easy for them to grab hold of. Before throwing the rope to your victim, shout to alert them that you are about to throw a rope. An inattentive victim is unlikely to be able to catch your rope.

The underarm throw: release the throw bag when your hand is pointing at the target.

Throw the bag with any style you find successful; the underarm throw is favoured for long distances while the overarm throw is preferred for shorter distances. Once the victim has a hold of the rope, crouch to form a low and stable position with your body and pendulum the victim in to the side.

When the victim is safely out of the water and away from danger, re-pack the rope into the bag so that it is ready to use again. Always check that your throw bag has been packed correctly before going to the river. If the rope is knotted or tangled it will not throw easily to the victim and may cause further difficulties instead of solving the problem.

⚠ When scouting rapids always carry your throw bag with you – there may not be enough time to rush back to your canoe to fetch it in an emergency. Carry your bag in your hand or on a quick release waist belt. Using a waist belt will reduce the chance of you ever forgetting your throw bag.

Practise throw bagging until you are confident of hitting your target first time every time. Start off in the garden aiming at the garden gnomes then progress to practising on the river with friends as victims. On a warm and sunny day, throw bag practice is a good excuse for a refreshing swim. You may only get one chance to get a rope to a victim as they float by, you could save their life.

Inspecting

Looking at what is ahead from a point of safety allows you to choose the most appropriate line down a rapid. If you proceed blindly, progress is risky. The term 'read and run' is used to describe rapids that can be paddled safely from eddy to eddy; from the start you can see a safe line to the next eddy and from the second eddy a safe line to the third, etc. This fluid style of paddling is favoured by many recreational canoeists as there is no need to interrupt the flow of the journey because you can't see where you are going.

If you can't see a clear or safe line down a rapid get out and inspect. The siphon on the river right was not visible from upstream.

If you arrive at a point where you cannot see a clear line to the next safe eddy, further inspection is necessary. The first option you have is to stand up in the canoe: the increase in height allows you to see much more of the river without having to climb out of the canoe and onto the river bank. If after standing up in the canoe the line is still unclear or you are still unsure of the best route, then you must get out of the canoe and walk downstream along the river bank to inspect the rapid.

The aim of inspecting is simple: to check it is safe for you and your friends to proceed down the river. Try not to get into lengthy discussions about the different lines and hazards. If you cannot see a safe line after an initial inspection, walking around is probably a safer option.

When inspecting a rapid always wear your helmet and carry your throw line. If you fall in the river the helmet will protect your head and if a friend falls in you can rescue them with your throw line.

Always look positively at a rapid. Focusing on the hazards will unnerve you and ultimately you will be psychologically drawn towards the big stopper you wanted to avoid. Instead, focus on where you want the boat to be.

⚠️ IF YOU CANNOT SEE A SAFE LINE STAND UP OR GET OUT AND HAVE A LOOK. NEVER FEEL EMBARRASSED TO STOP AND INSPECT. A FEW MINUTES INVESTED IN INSPECTING MAY SAVE A NASTY SWIM AND A FEW HOURS RESCUING A PINNED CANOE.

Breaking in and breaking out

Paddling your canoe out of the eddy and into the flowing water (breaking in) is an exhilarating experience, whether it is your first time or you have done it a thousand times before. As soon as you feel the force of the water on the hull of the canoe the journey begins and the adventure down the river starts. Before breaking in to the flow you should do two things: look downstream to plan where you are going and look upstream for oncoming paddlers or other hazards floating towards you.

Paddling out of the flowing water and into an eddy (breaking out) is a key skill for every paddler to master; it will allow you to safely stop during your journey down the river.

To break in to the flow first accelerate the canoe out of the eddy, turn your head to look downstream, lean into the turn and use your paddle for support and to control the turn. This sequence shows a cross bow rudder being used to turn the canoe.

There is no exact formula to work out the optimum angle at which you need to exit an eddy and break in to the flow; experiment and learn. Start with the canoe pointing at 45 degrees to the oncoming flow and take a few quick paddle strokes to accelerate the canoe out of the eddy, across the eddy line and into the flow. The key to successful break-ins is using your head; as you paddle out of the eddy look towards the front of the canoe and as you cross the eddy line turn your head to look downstream. Turning your head does two very important things: firstly, you are able to look where you are going and secondly, turning your head will automatically transfer weight from your upstream knee to your downstream knee. The transfer of weight lifts the upstream edge of the canoe out of the water and reduces the risk of a capsize.

Keep your head looking towards your goal eddy. As the canoe turns towards the eddy, redistribute your weight equally between your knees so the hull of the canoe is flat and the front is pointing towards your goal eddy.

Many different paddle strokes can be used to break in to the flow; the choice depends on whether you paddle solo or tandem and left or right. Any turning stroke can be used to break in, e.g. forward sweep strokes, bow and cross bow rudders and bow and cross bow draws are particularly effective.

Tandem paddlers have a slightly harder task than solo paddlers as they must work together. The application of the teamwork skills learnt during the basic and intermediate paddle strokes is crucial. Before you leave the eddy, talk through your plan so you both know what to do and where you are going. Both paddlers should turn their heads and lean into the turn.

Once in rapids you need to be able to paddle back into an eddy; this is known as breaking out. A skilful canoeist will aim to attain many eddies on the way down a rapid to achieve a controlled descent. Breaking out of the flow into an eddy is almost the same action as breaking in and the same tips apply.

WHEN OUT ON THE RIVER PRACTISING YOUR BREAK-INS AND -OUTS, TRY TURNING THE CANOE AROUND AND ENTERING AND LEAVING EDDIES BACKWARDS. THE TECHNIQUE IS EXACTLY THE SAME AS THE FORWARDS MANOEUVRE. PRACTISING REVERSE BREAK-INS AND -OUTS CAN TRANSFORM AN UNCHALLENGING SECTION OF RIVER INTO A NEW AND EXCITING TRAINING ENVIRONMENT.

The key to successful break-outs is turning your head; as you approach the eddy keep your eyes looking towards the top of the eddy. Approach the eddy at an angle of approximately 45 degrees at a speed slightly quicker than that of the water. As you cross the eddy line lift the weight off your downstream knee and lean into the turn.

If you have timed your break-out well and approached with enough speed, you should not need a paddle stroke to bring the canoe into the eddy. The addition of a paddle stroke will guarantee the break-out and assist with balancing the turn. The paddle stroke should be initiated with the paddle blade in the eddy. If the stroke is started with the paddle in the flow, or in the eddy line, it may hinder the break-out.

Three tips (in order of priority) for breaking in and out: first is to turn your head and look into the turn, second is to lean the canoe into the turn and third is to use your paddle to assist with the turning motion and provide an extra balance point should it be needed.

Ferry gliding

Ferry gliding uses the power of the water to push the canoe from one side of the river to the other without travelling downstream. The name ferry gliding is taken from the old technique used by ferries or rafts to traverse fast-flowing rivers. A rope was spanned across the river and the ferry attached to it by two short ropes, so that it floated at an angle of 45 degrees to the oncoming current. The oncoming water is deflected off the upstream side of the ferry and the result is that the ferry is pushed across the river.

For a perfect example of ferry gliding watch the way a duck crosses a flowing river. The duck sets itself at a slight angle to the flow and paddles forwards against the flow. The combination of the duck paddling upstream at an angle and the flow of water moves the duck sideways across the river.

To ferry glide a canoe across a flowing river you need to consider two related factors: the speed of the flow and the angle of the canoe. The faster the flow, the steeper the angle you will need to cross the flow in order to avoid losing ground.

Set the canoe up in the eddy with the front pointing upstream. Make a few powerful strokes to accelerate the canoe out of the eddy and into the flow. As you cross the eddy line slightly lift the upstream edge of the canoe to prevent it catching in the oncoming flow. Maintain the angle of the canoe in the flow by using forward paddle strokes. If you really have to fight to hold the angle then it is too big and if you are not travelling across the river then the angle is too small. When ferry gliding, it is easiest to apply most of the paddle strokes on the downstream side of the canoe. Solo paddlers should swap sides or use cross-deck paddle strokes. When you reach the eddy on the other side of the river, apply a little extra power to cross the eddy line. As you cross into the eddy, turn the canoe so it is facing upstream.

Reverse ferry gliding is a very useful skill for moving water canoeists. The theory is exactly the same as forwards ferry gliding. The angle must be set to match the speed of the water and downstream paddle strokes are needed to maintain the angle of the canoe in the flow. When you are paddling down a rapid and need to change direction away from a hazard, simply reverse ferry glide away. Back paddling will slow the canoe down and give you more time to react, and the ferry glide will move the canoe away from the hazard.

Experience is the best tool for selecting the best angle to ferry glide across a flowing river. If in doubt start with a smaller angle than you think is necessary, as it is much easier to increase the angle than reduce it when ferry gliding. Take every trip to the river as an opportunity to practise your ferry glides. Watch other paddlers and analyse the angle and paddle strokes they use.

The S cross

S cross is the name given to a combination move of break-in and break-out. Break in to the flow and travel downstream to the next safe eddy on the other side of the river, where you break out of the flow. The resulting path of travel would look like an S rotated ninety degrees when viewed from above. The S cross is a great way to make safe and controlled progress down a river. It is also a great way of practising your break-ins and break-outs.

One of the keys to success when performing an S cross is good edge control and awareness. When leaving the eddy you should lean downstream into the turn. As the canoe travels across the flow the canoe should be flat and then as you break out you should lean upstream into the turn as you enter the eddy.

When you leave the eddy turn your head to look downstream at your goal eddy; the canoe will turn towards the eddy. As you cross the eddy line of the goal eddy, turn your head to look at the top of the eddy and use a paddle stroke to assist you in attaining the eddy.

Surfing

Standing waves can be found on every whitewater river in the world and surfing a wave with your canoe is one of the great pleasures of whitewater paddling. Standing waves vary in size and suitability for surfing with a canoe. Start with a small easily accessible wave before building up to bigger, more challenging, waves.

There are two ways to catch a surf wave: either drop in on the wave from upstream or ferry glide out of a convenient eddy. Ferry gliding out from an eddy is easier than dropping in from upstream. To paddle onto a wave from an eddy, position your canoe facing upstream and paddle powerfully out of the eddy. Keep your head looking upstream, the canoe pointing against the flow and the hull of the canoe flat on the water. To surf the canoe must maintain its position on the face of the wave; you may need to help the canoe by paddling a little at the start of the surf.

Ferry glide out of the eddy and across onto the wave. Turn your head and use your paddle to carve the canoe from one side of the wave to the other.

Suddenly you will feel the power of the water take over and the canoe will be surfing all on its own – it is an incredible feeling. If the front of the canoe starts to dig into the oncoming water lean back slightly. If you feel you are falling off the back of the wave, shift your weight slightly forwards. To maintain the front surf keep the canoe parallel to the direction of the current and the hull flat on the water. Control the surf using a stern rudder to hold the canoe in a front surf.

Once you have established a front surf you may want to ride the wave and carve across its face. To carve across the face of a wave you must apply an edge to the canoe. Keep your head looking upstream and experiment with subtle weight shifts from left to right. More weight on your right knee will turn the canoe right. To bring the canoe back into a front surf, lift your weight off the right knee and push down briefly on the left. As the canoe turns to front surf, balance your weight equally.

Use your head: turning your head influences the direction in which the canoe turns. When you look straight ahead your weight is evenly distributed between your left and right sides and the canoe floats with the hull flat on the water. When you turn your head, you transfer more weight onto the side you turn to. This in turn affects the way the canoe is balanced; the lighter side lifts up and the heavier side digs deeper into the water. The resulting change in balance turns the canoe in the direction you have turned your head. To go left, first look left.

Style and smile: the two key ingredients for a great day at the river.

To exit the wave when you are finished surfing, turn your head to look downstream and apply edge. The canoe will begin to turn and then fall off the back of the wave. Use a paddle stroke to help turn the canoe until it is pointing in the direction you want to paddle.

With style and a smile

When out on the river there is one trick guaranteed to improve your performance: paddle your canoe with style and a smile. A stylish canoeist kneels proudly in the canoe with good posture, and uses efficient paddle strokes to manoeuvre the canoe deliberately from eddy to eddy. A smiling canoeist is a happy canoeist, and happy canoeists are the best type of paddlers. They are enjoying themselves and bringing a friendly vibe to the river. Whatever you are doing, do it with style and a smile.

ROLLING

Rolling a canoe in whitewater requires self-confidence. Train and practise thoroughly, and enjoy the rewards when you roll up for the first time in anger.

The Eskimo roll and open canoeing are not often associated. However, there is no reason why a skilled paddler in a suitably outfitted canoe should not roll after a capsize. Being able to roll your canoe is a key to paddling challenging whitewater rivers or improving your playboating skills at your local wave. Once mastered, a reliable roll is a skill that will aid your progression as an OC1 or OC2 (open canoe, one- or two-person) paddler.

The warm and clear water in a swimming pool will help you to progress quickly when learning to roll an open canoe.

Learning to roll your canoe is best done in the comfort of a swimming pool. The warm, clear water will help you to progress swiftly. Find a friend who wants to roll a canoe and learn together; two heads are better than one and empathy is great for motivation and learning. Being able to watch, help and discuss with a friend will speed up your learning and make the experience more enjoyable.

One of the key factors to appreciate when learning to roll your canoe is the outfitting. To have any real chance of successfully rolling your canoe it should be fitted with fully inflated airbags, a saddle, foot rests, knee blocks and possibly hip pads and thigh straps. Outfitting should be comfortable and not hinder the entry or exit from the canoe.

This canoe is outfitted with a bulkhead saddle system, hip pads and quick-release thigh straps.

The height of the saddle is important to consider when paddling and learning to roll an OC1. If it's too low, the canoe will be uncomfortable to sit in for long periods. If the saddle is too high, raising your centre of gravity, it will make the canoe feel very unstable. The ideal saddle height varies from paddler to paddler depending on your leg length and your flexibility; as a rough guide, twenty-two centimetres high is a good starting point.

Airbags should be fully inflated and attached using deck lashing and anchor straps. Foot rests are not essential but if you choose to use them they should be adjusted to fit comfortably. Thigh straps or a lap strap provide both advantages and disadvantages for the canoe paddler; straps provide increased contact and control over the canoe, therefore assisting with rolling and more advanced manoeuvres. However, a strap system should not put off the beginner. If you do not feel confident with straps do not use them; it is possible to roll a canoe without a strap system.

Wearing a helmet and buoyancy aid helps replicate what you will experience when out on the river.

When learning or practising your rolling skills it is best to do so in a situation as close to real life as possible. On the river you will be wearing your buoyancy aid and helmet. During learning and training sessions you should also wear your buoyancy aid and helmet, as this will increase your chances of rolling successfully when you capsize for real on the river.

⚠ Before starting to learn to roll, be sure you fit comfortably in your canoe and that you can quickly and safely exit it both above and below water. If you choose to use a strap system be sure it is fitted with quick-release buckles and that you are able to release them quickly and easily every time. Straps without a quick release mechanism should never be used.

Solo canoe rolling

The first step when learning to roll is to practise the rolling movement; this is best done using the side of the swimming pool. Hold onto the poolside with both hands and start to tip the canoe slowly over towards the side. Keep your arms outstretched at ninety degrees to the canoe and your body floating on the surface of the water. Hold your body in position with pressure from your hands on the poolside and support the canoe with your knees and hips. To roll the canoe back upright apply pressure with your knees and a rolling/twisting motion with your hips, slowly turning the canoe back upright. Aim to keep your body floating on the surface and your head underwater for the duration. To finish the roll, lean your body forward and over the front of the canoe. Focus on keeping your head low and aligned with your spine.

Use the poolside to help you learn the body movement. Keep your arms straight and at ninety degrees to the canoe. Your head should come up out of the water last.

The movement of your head is the key to successful rolling. The head is the heaviest part of your body and should therefore be the last part of your body to leave the water. Your brain will naturally tell you to get your head out of the water first. Try to ignore this impulse and concentrate on rolling the canoe up first, then bringing your body over the front of the canoe and then lifting your head. By keeping your head low beside your forearms or the paddle shaft, you will improve the performance of your roll.

Once you have mastered the rolling movement with two hands, try rolling up using only one hand.

Practise until you feel confident with the movement and you can perform the poolside roll with ease. Try using only one hand to support yourself during the roll or even just a few fingers. To start with you might tip the canoe just ninety degrees, or maybe even just forty-five degrees, then work up to completely capsizing the canoe and rolling it back up again. Progress at a rate you feel comfortable with; rushing will not speed up or improve your learning.

Learn to roll and practise rolling on both sides.

The on-side roll

Having mastered the poolside rolling movement you are now ready to progress to using a paddle. To begin, ask a friend to hold the paddle blade in position as you practise. The paddle should float on the surface of the water at ninety degrees to the side of the canoe. Your friend can support the paddle blade from beneath and keep it from moving sideways or underwater too much. As with the poolside roll capsize towards the paddle, and wait until the canoe has settled upside down. Float your body to the surface of the water, roll the canoe upright using your knees and hips then, to finish, recover your body over the front of the canoe. Use your paddle to support your body weight during the roll. Practise this roll on both sides until you can roll without the help of your friend.

Get a friend to help support and guide your paddle as you learn to roll; this will speed up your progress and reduce frustration and confusion.

Ask your friend for feedback and try to learn from your mistakes. To improve your learning experience, set up a video camera on the poolside and record your training. What you think you are doing is often slightly different from what you are actually doing. This is why the roll sometimes might not work when you think you are doing everything correctly.

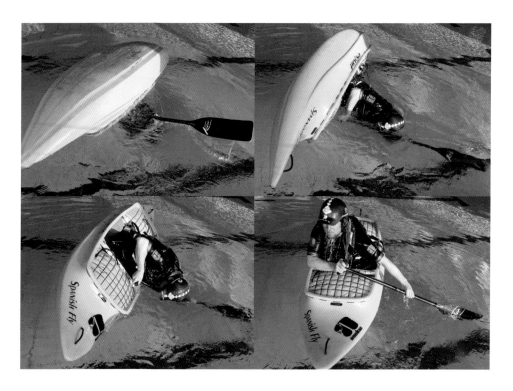

The half roll: capsize towards the paddle, wait until the canoe has settled, float your body to the surface, roll the canoe up using your hips and knees then recover using the paddle. Remember, your head should come up last.

When the pre-set-up half roll has been mastered, it is time to move onto the crux of the roll, i.e. setting up to roll underwater. You will now be familiar with the starting position for the roll: canoe settled upside down, body floating on the surface and paddle outstretched at a ninety degree angle to the canoe.

Take your time to orientate yourself underwater and find the start position for the roll. Some people find using a nose clip and/or swimming goggles helps them to relax underwater, allowing them to concentrate fully on performing the roll.

A complete Eskimo roll: capsize and wait for the canoe to settle, reach up to the surface of the water with the paddle, float your body on the paddle and roll up the canoe and, finally, lift you body and head out of the water and over the front of the canoe.

Once you have found your start position for the roll, perform the roll as you have practised: it is that easy. The first successful roll should be the start of many. Practise on both sides and capsizing in different positions, setting up and rolling back up again.

During your practice do not expect to succeed at every attempt. In the beginning, rolling takes a lot of energy and concentration. Understand when it is time to stop and have a break. This is normally when you are fed up with trying and not succeeding. Use this time to review your progress on the video camera and have a drink of water.

The off-side roll

Once you have mastered the on-side roll the next step is the off-side roll. The off-side roll is a key skill for any paddler who intends to play in stoppers or tackle hard whitewater. The purpose of this roll is to enable the paddler to roll up on the off- (non-paddle) side of the canoe without swapping the grip on the paddle underwater.

Off-side roll: reach up to the surface with the paddle, push the paddle blade downwards and towards the front of the canoe, twist the paddle blade to finish the roll and recover with a cross deck forward paddle stroke.

IT REQUIRES A FAIR AMOUNT OF POWER AND COORDINATION TO SUCCEED, SO TRY IT ONCE YOU HAVE ALREADY MASTERED THE ON-SIDE ROLL.

The movement is essentially the same as an on-side canoe roll, performed back to front. Wait for the canoe to settle and float your body to the surface, positioning the paddle at ninety degrees to the canoe. The aim is to finish the roll with the paddle blade flat on the surface of the water towards the front of the canoe with the paddle shaft parallel to the off-side of the canoe and the T grip by your hip. To gain extra support when finishing the roll, many paddlers perform an off-side power stroke or sweep stroke directly after the roll to be sure of staying upright and in control. The rolling action for the body and the canoe is the same as for an on-side roll except in the other direction. Roll the canoe using pressure from your knees and hips and support your body weight with the paddle. Aim to finish the roll with your body forwards over the front of the canoe. The off-side roll is one of the trickiest rolls to master in canoe paddling, and you should not expect instant success during your training sessions.

The hand roll

Next up in the canoeist's box of tricks is the hand roll (a roll with very little purpose for the canoeist other than to show off, but we all like to show off from time to time!) The rolling motion is the same as for every roll: capsize and wait for the canoe to settle upside down, float your body to the surface and reach your hands out at ninety degrees from the canoe as far as possible. Use your knees and hips to roll the canoe up while supporting the weight of your body on your hands. Recover forwards with your body weight over the front of the canoe. Unlike rolling with a paddle, you need to get your head out of the water quickly and on the other side of the canoe. A few extra splashes with the hands often help to get the boat back upright at the end of the roll. Keep your body weight low and forwards during the roll and apply as much power as possible with your knees and hips.

Capsize and float your body to the surface and reach as far out as you can with your hands. Roll the canoe with your hips and knees and wave your hands powerfully from one side to the other like a Mexican wave. Get your head across to the other side of the canoe and support with your hands to finish the roll.

Learning to roll takes time, patience and energy, so do not try to do too much in one go. Take regular breaks, review your progress on the video and talk with your learning partner. If you are tired, stop – you will only frustrate yourself and make little progress by carrying on.

Tandem canoe rolling

The key to success in tandem canoeing is communication. Before learning and practising your rolling, make a plan and be sure both paddlers understand it.

AS WITH LEARNING TO ROLL A SOLO CANOE, TIME SPENT USING THE POOLSIDE TO PRACTISE AND GET A FEEL FOR THE TIMING OF THE ROLL WILL BE WELL SPENT, AS WILL USING A VIDEO TO RECORD AND ANALYSE YOUR PROGRESS. DRAFTING IN ANOTHER FRIEND TO OBSERVE AND PROVIDE FEEDBACK WILL ALSO BE BENEFICIAL.

When rolling a tandem canoe the challenge of learning to roll is matched by the challenge of working flawlessly as a team underwater while holding your breath. The techniques learnt to roll a solo canoe can be transferred directly to tandem canoe: the on-side, off-side and hand rolling techniques used are exactly the same. Timing and coordination are needed; without either a successful roll will be more luck than judgement.

To work as a team you need a prearranged plan; communicating and planning underwater is not an option. I recommend that the front paddler takes the lead and the back paddler follows, as the front paddler generally has a more complicated set-up and therefore will generally take longer. There are two techniques that can be used by a tandem canoe crew to roll: the front paddler can swap hand positions on the paddle or can perform an off-side roll. Once the front paddler has set up they should start to roll. When the back paddler feels the roll starting, they should start their roll.

Front paddler, swapping hands roll

As the canoe capsizes both paddlers should start to think about the roll. As the canoe settles upside down, the back paddler floats their body to the surface and reaches out with their paddle at ninety degrees to the canoe and waits. The front paddler swaps their hands over on the paddle so they are now holding the paddle on the same side as the back paddler. There are many varying techniques to swapping paddle sides underwater, with the common theme of not letting go of the paddle with more than one hand at a time. Float your body to the surface as normal, reach out with the paddle and start to roll. When the back paddler feels the front paddler start to roll, they should start. The paddlers should then roll the canoe together. This roll has the advantage of being very powerful as both paddlers are using the strong on-side roll on the same side. However, swapping the paddle grip underwater can take time and be tricky. Swapping hands also increases the chance of losing grip on the paddle and losing it completely. The front paddler will also need to swap hands again once you are upright to continue paddling; this can also cause problems in the middle of a tricky rapid or manoeuvre.

The back paddler waits until the front paddler has swapped their hands around and starts to roll; the back paddler then follows. Both paddlers perform a normal on-side roll.

Front paddler, off-side roll

The other option is for the front paddler to perform an off-side roll. The set-up, roll and recovery can all be performed quicker and the chance of losing the paddle is considerably reduced. The disadvantage is that the front paddler is using a slightly less powerful roll. A good tandem canoe crew should be able to perform this roll combination successfully in most, if not all, situations.

The front paddler performs an off-side roll and the back paddler rolls normally. When the canoe has completely capsized the front paddler starts the roll and the back paddler follows.

Each paddler sets up to roll as normal: wait for the canoe to settle, float your body to the surface and reach out with the paddles at ninety degrees to the canoe. The front paddler should initiate the roll and the back paddler should follow. After successfully completing the roll, the front paddler can swap back onto their on-side without the need to swap their grip on the paddle again.

A hand roll in a tandem whitewater canoe is rarely seen. A powerful and synchronised rolling action is needed from both paddlers, and a little bit of luck!

The tandem hand roll

If the hand roll struggles to justify itself as a useful technique, then hand rolling an OC2 is surely a trick only good for impressing onlookers. First, and most importantly, decide which side you are going to roll on then try, try and try again. The technique for hand rolling is the same, with added strength and determination.

Rolling in control

Rolling in anger on whitewater can be very different from practising in the pool. The water is no longer clear and warm and is a lot more turbulent. Do not let this put you off. Once you have learnt to roll in the pool, take every trip on the river as an opportunity to practise your roll. Practice is the one thing that will undoubtedly improve your rolling. Do not be put off by swims: learn from them.

Everytime you successfully roll up it is a good feeling, your first roll following an accidental capsize is the best feeling. Rolling up in turbulent water when pushing your limits regenerates the feeling of your first roll, "Yes! I've made it."

Rolling your canoe is a useful skill to master for any aspiring whitewater OC1 or OC2 paddler (better still is learning not to capsize). Learning to roll will certainly improve your balance and the quality of your bracing strokes, directly reducing your chance of capsizing. One issue worth bearing in mind is that if you are on a shallow or very rocky river and are not rolling well, it is best to quickly eject from the canoe. A swim could save you from a very sore head or maybe even a trip to the dentist.

To roll consistently and successfully requires practice, determination and the confidence to keep a clear head underwater. Orientate yourself underwater and set up calmly and confidently to roll. If you don't succeed on your first attempt but still have air in your lungs, set up and try again. Good luck!

COMPETITION

Taking part in a competition is a thrilling experience. The adrenalin and the cheers from the crowd help you to perform at your very best.

Human beings are competitive by nature and for many there is no better feeling than that of competing against others in sport. There are several competitive disciplines for open canoes, ranging from flat water sprint racing to whitewater freestyle. This chapter explores the competitive side of canoeing, how to prepare and train for competitions and what to expect at a typical event.

It is perfectly feasible to just turn up and compete, do your best and have fun. However, for those with more serious aspirations as a competition canoeist, a training programme should be considered to maximise potential. Physical and mental preparation are crucial for success. Just as important is a healthy diet and a sound knowledge of the rules of the sport.

Healthy living

During exercise, training and competition the body needs energy; this energy is provided by food and drink. First and most important is to keep your body hydrated. A normal adult male requires between two and three litres of water per day and when you are exercising or in a hot environment this amount should increase. Drinking water is good for you. There are many sports drinks available which help the body prepare, perform and recover from exercise. Whenever you go to the river to paddle, whether to train or not, always take a drink with you. Thirsty canoeists do not perform as well.

Leading a healthy lifestyle is important for many reasons. Anybody who aspires to win competitions should prioritise health. You should eat well, drink lots of water and take daily exercise.

A balanced diet will provide the body with good fuel to perform at its best. This fuel should be supplied in the form of a variety of different food types. Food can be classified into four groups: carbohydrates, proteins, fats and vitamins. A good diet should consist of a mix of all of these food types.

Base your diet on starchy foods. Each meal should be approximately one-third starchy food. Eat as much fruit and vegetables as possible, at least five portions per day. Eat more fish: it is a great source of protein, vitamins and minerals. Reduce your sugar and saturated fat intake. Drink more water. Never, ever, skip breakfast.

Know the game

Competitions are moderated by trained judges who know the rules of the sport inside out. If you want to succeed, learn the rules and learn how to use them to your advantage.

Before training for any type of competition it is important to understand what you are training for. If you do not know how you will be judged it is very difficult to prepare effectively for the competition. Read the rules so you understand how the competition will run. Join a local club or seek out special coaching from qualified and experienced experts. Their knowledge will help you to progress quickly and effectively.

Mental preparation

Focused on the finish line.

The fittest athlete with the best equipment will not perform at their best if not focused on the competition. The key to successful performance is maintaining a calm, confident and focused mind.

Mental imagery is a technique many competitors adopt to focus the mind. Before the race or ride imagine yourself performing at your best and try to focus on the feelings of success and euphoria that your body develops when it has performed at its best. Imagine standing on top of the winners' podium or crossing the finish line first.

Physical training

To perform at your best the body needs to be in top shape and ready to give 100% effort. Before any kind of strenuous activity, a warm-up is recommended to reduce the likelihood of injury. Canoeing is no exception. When you have finished exercising you should warm down to prevent cramps and muscle stiffness and to relax after exerting your body.

A serious competitor will cross-train using activities other than canoeing. Swimming is a superb low-impact exercise that will improve both strength and stamina.

To optimise your training you need to determine a goal: what are you training for and why? Each competitive discipline has different demands on the body; a marathon racer needs a different fitness from a whitewater freestyle competitor. To maximise your training time, make a training plan with time frames to achieve specific goals and to measure and record performance. If your aim is to train for a specific competition, allow time to rest in the few days before the competition. Overtraining can be as hazardous to top performance as insufficient training. Strength, stamina and flexibility are the three main areas to focus on during your training sessions. Aim to build up the muscle groups you will use during competition; the stronger you are, the better you can perform. Stamina and general fitness are crucial to success. If you are exhausted half-way through a race the chance of winning is vastly reduced. A flexible body will perform better than a stiff body; stretching will increase the range of movement and reduce the chance of injury.

Competitions are fun and you should enjoy being on the water with your fellow competitors. Here Jez, Toby and I enjoy the whitewater freestyle World Cup final.

 The most important factor to focus on when training and competing is to enjoy yourself. If you are not having fun, your body and mind will be tense and stressed and you will not be able to perform at your best. Smile: it makes everything more fun.

Open canoe competitive disciplines

Sprint and marathon racing

The first form of competitive canoeing was racing, either over short distances (sprint) or long distances (marathon). Sprint racing is one of the two canoeing disciplines that feature in the modern Olympic Games; competitors race over 500 and 1000 metre courses in either single or tandem high kneeling racing canoes.

(Left) two OC1 competitors battle it out in the annual Devises to Westminster canoe race. (Right) a high kneeling racing canoe is the fastest of all racing canoes, but also the most difficult to paddle due to the high centre of gravity and narrow kneeling stance.

It is possible to enter a race using any canoe or paddle but there are specific designs for racing that will increase performance potential. A typical racing canoe will be long and narrow with no rocker and a rounded or V shaped hull. These design factors maximise the potential top speed of a canoe. Canoes designed specifically for racing are made from composite materials to minimise the weight of the canoe. Lighter canoes go quicker on the water and are easier to portage.

Racing canoes can be subdivided into two categories: high kneeling canoes and sit and switch canoes. High kneeling canoes are the fastest type of racing canoe, recognisable by the high kneeling paddling position. These canoes are very fast but can be very unstable for novice racing paddlers. Sit and switch canoes are similar in appearance to a standard open canoe. The paddlers sit and should often switch paddling sides during racing and training.

A cranked paddle. note the change in angle between the shaft and paddle blade and the shape of the paddle blade.

Racing canoes are subject to maximum length and minimum weight restrictions. These restrictions vary from class to class but are only really applicable to paddlers competing at the very top of the sport. Most general purpose canoes will not infringe the racing rules.

For high kneeling racing canoes paddlers use large bladed, straight shafted paddles normally made from composite material such as carbon. Sit and switch paddlers tend to use a short paddle with a cranked shaft. The difference in paddle designs is due to the different sitting positions in the different types of racing canoes.

Many expert racing paddlers choose not to wear a buoyancy aid during training and competitions, as this enables them to regulate their body temperature better and therefore perform better. For marathon races, most paddlers wear a hydration system to allow for hands-free drinking during the race.

The skills needed to participate in a canoe race are fairly basic. A paddler should be of reasonable fitness and be able to paddle in a straight line efficiently. Sprint and marathon racing is a great way to keep fit and improve your forward paddling technique. To compete at the highest level, a well-developed forward stroke is required to maximise power and efficiency. Paddlers should have an optimised power to weight ratio to ensure they travel as quickly as possible. High kneeling canoe racers must have good balance and a powerful forward stroke as they use the whole body to pull the paddle through the water. Sit and switch canoe racers frequently swap paddling sides so the crew must develop a strategy to minimise loss of paddle stroke rate. Experienced canoe crews can swap sides without a drop in the stroke rate.

A tandem crew portaging during a race, a key skill to master for all serious marathon racers.

Competitors may need to portage locks or weirs during marathon races, which involves jumping out of the canoe, running around an obstacle, getting back in and getting back up to speed. Portages have become a crucial part of every serious racer's training schedule.

There are several very high profile international canoe races that are open to all paddlers with suitable experience. The Devises to Westminster race covers a 125-mile course along the Kennet and

Avon canal and the River Thames in England. Competitors can race straight through in one go, or race over stages during the four-day Easter weekend. With a history of over fifty years of racing, the Devises to Westminster is the highlight for many marathon racers. The Arctic Canoe Race challenges paddlers to race 325 miles along the River Torne in Scandinavia. This is one of the most gruelling canoe races in the world. Fast flowing rapids, waves and icy cold water push competitors to the limits of physical endurance.

Whitewater freestyle

Whitewater freestyle or rodeo is one of the most dynamic canoe disciplines. Paddlers in small one-person canoes perform tricks while surfing waves or stoppers. The sport first developed during the late 1980s when whitewater paddlers started to play on waves and stoppers on their way down the river. The sport is progressing very quickly with paddlers surfing bigger waves and performing gravity-defying tricks that were previously not thought possible.

Front surfing a wave to set up for a big trick. Front surfing is a key skill to master for whitewater freestyle.

Canoe paddlers compete in the OC1 category using specifically designed freestyle canoes. The design of these canoes is controlled by rules to prevent the class from turning into the closed cockpit C1 class. Competitors must kneel in the canoe and use a single bladed paddle. There are also rules governing the amount of extra flotation competitors are allowed to add to their canoe, the height of the cockpit and the amount of open area on the deck to try to keep the canoes looking like canoes (and not like kayaks).

OC1 paddlers are very much in the minority in the whitewater freestyle scene. The canoe is not the easiest craft to use to perform the latest tricks and, as a consequence, the canoe class has fewer entrants. Those who do compete are very passionate about the sport and are determined to keep the discipline alive.

Big tricks are the name of the game in top flight freestyle competitions.

Paddlers wishing to try their hand at whitewater freestyle should have good basic whitewater skills and be able to confidently ferry glide across currents and surf small waves and stoppers. The ability to roll your canoe will reduce the time spent swimming down the river; whitewater freestyle is a great way to practise your rolling. Proficient whitewater freestyle canoeists have good balance and edge control to position the canoe on the wave, flexibility and strength to move the canoe around the wave and launch it into the air and, most importantly, the desire to have fun paddling.

The cartwheel is a basic freestyle move. The canoe and paddler rotate 360 degrees in the vertical plane.

Any whitewater canoe can be surfed on small waves but to really get involved in whitewater freestyle, a specifically designed canoe will be needed. The latest whitewater freestyle canoes are made from composite material or moulded in plastic, allowing designers to make complex designs and reduce the weight of the canoe. Whitewater freestyle canoes feature planing hulls and sharp edges to allow dynamic surfing across the face of the wave to set up dynamic moves. The slicey ends can be easily pushed underwater to perform vertical moves and the volume in the middle of the canoe helps it to leap into the air for aerial moves. Whitewater freestyle canoes are fitted with big airbags to keep as much water out of the canoe as possible; this keeps the canoe light and easy to move about the wave. The outfitting of whitewater freestyle is key to top performance. The paddler must be well fitted to the canoe to allow every movement of the body to be transferred to the canoe; a loose fit in the canoe makes it difficult to perform tricks. Many paddlers fit thigh straps and hip pads into the canoe for optimum control and performance.

Before going paddling ensure that you fit comfortably into your canoe and that you can quickly and safely exit your canoe both above and below water in case of an emergency. If you choose to use a strap system, be sure it is fitted with quick release buckles and that you are able to release them quickly and with ease every time. A strap system without a quick release mechanism should never be used.

Many paddlers enter the OC1 at freestyle events just for fun. It has a reputation as a very relaxed event with competitors helping each other out and encouraging each other. The easiest way to get involved in OC1 freestyle is to approach a paddler at your local playspot or at a competition. They will no doubt be more than happy to explain a bit more about the sport and let you have a go in their canoe.

Open canoe slalom

Open canoe slalom is similar to any other kind of slalom: competitors must navigate through a course of gates without touching or missing any. The winner is the paddler who sets the quickest time without incurring any penalties.

The aim of open canoe slalom is to navigate a course of gates as quickly as possible without incurring any penalties.

Slalom canoeing was developed by European slalom skiers looking for a similar sport for the summer months and open canoes were first used in slaloms during the 1930s. As the sport progressed, the closed cockpit C1s and C2s were developed to allow canoe slalom paddlers to perform trickier manoeuvres on more challenging courses. The emergence of these specifically designed slalom canoes meant the open canoe disappeared from the European slalom scene.

The sport of open canoe slalom re-emerged during the early 1980s in the USA and is still going strong. There are three different categories in modern day open canoe slalom: a recreational class for paddlers using general purpose commercially available whitewater canoes (REC), a racing class for paddlers using canoes specially designed for open canoe slalom racing (RAC), and an experimental class (X) to allow innovative paddlers to present new designs for slalom canoes that do not fit either the REC or RAC category.

Slalom canoes are sparsely outfitted to keep weight to a bare minimum; small foam saddles and lightweight straps, airbags and wooden gunwales all help to keep the canoe weight down and maximise the performance potential. There are separate classes for X, recreational and racing canoes, for solo and tandem canoes and for men's, ladies, juniors and mixed crews. All classes must conform to a set of rules governing the shape and weight of the canoes, to ensure that the boats used are recognisable as open canoes and are safe to be paddled on the river.

An open canoe slalom course should not be longer than 410 metres and will feature between 20 and 25 slalom gates. There are two types of gates in slalom: downstream and upstream. A downstream gate is identified by green and white stripes and competitors should paddle downstream through the gate. An upstream gate is identified by red and white stripes and competitors must paddle upstream through the gate. A course should feature a minimum of five upstream gates. The course will be set out with a reasonable split between left and right manoeuvres to prevent paddlers who prefer a specific side having an advantage. The course should not put competitors or their equipment in any unnecessary danger.

The aim of open canoe slalom is to faultlessly negotiate the course in the fastest time possible. If errors are made, extra seconds are added to the time. A ten second penalty is awarded when a competitor paddles through the gate but touches one or both of the poles with his or her body, paddle or canoe. A fifty second penalty is awarded if a competitor misses a gate completely or touches a pole and misses the gate.

Open canoe slalom is a sport intended to be accessible to all whitewater canoe paddlers. Any whitewater canoe can be used in the REC class as long as it is outfitted with airbags and end grabs and all paddlers should wear a buoyancy aid and helmet and use a single bladed paddle. Open canoe slalom courses are designed so a smooth and flowing run through the gates is achievable for the better competitors in each class but not impossible for beginners, allowing all paddlers to enjoy their runs at the event.

Flat water freestyle

Flat water freestyle, or canoe ballet as it is sometimes known, is a genre of open canoeing based on the flat water paddling techniques of Native Americans. The aim of flat water freestyle is to perform graceful manoeuvres by using efficient paddle strokes combined with precise canoe control.

A tandem crew performing flat water freestyle: the aim is move the canoe as gracefully as possible.

Any paddler can try flat water freestyle by focusing on using efficient paddle strokes and moving the canoe gracefully over the water. The skills needed to become involved are no more than those needed to paddle an open canoe on flat water.

Open canoes designed for flat water freestyle are lightweight and easy to manoeuvre, slightly smaller than a general purpose open canoe and with little rocker. Solo flat water freestyle canoes are sparsely outfitted and often do not have seats fitted. Flat water freestyle canoes tend to be made of wood; this choice of material enables light and visually beautiful canoes to be constructed. The choice of paddle is also important; a wooden deep water touring paddle such as an otter tail will allow for much better execution of the paddle strokes required for flat water freestyle. Many paddlers also use a foam kneeling mat on the hull of the canoe to increase comfort during long periods of kneeling.

During some competitions it is not compulsory to wear a buoyancy aid. Competitions are held on sheltered water where help is close at hand and the lack of buoyancy aid allows the competitors greater freedom of movement.

Flat water freestyle canoes are slightly smaller and lighter than general purpose canoes and sparsely outfitted to save weight. Note the foam mat on the hull to make kneeling for long periods of time more comfortable.

The competitive version of flat water freestyle is interpretive freestyle. Competitors in either solo or tandem open canoes perform routines to music; imagine synchronised swimming or ice dancing. The routine must be performed within a set area (thirty by fifty metres) and is judged using five categories: technical difficulty, technical execution, compulsory manoeuvres, choreography and showmanship. The aim of competition is to demonstrate a graceful and efficient paddling style that is in harmony with the choice of music. Freestyle canoeists aim to utilise all variations of paddle strokes and aim to perform manoeuvres both forwards and backwards and on both sides of the canoe.

Skilled paddlers can turn the canoe smoothly and dynamically with minimum effort. Teamwork plays a large part in successful tandem flat water freestyle canoeing.

Flat water freestyle is a discipline of open canoeing in its infancy and every year more people get involved and the sport grows. The scene is biggest in North America, where there are annual symposiums and workshops and even a national championship. In Europe the scene is smaller, with only one event annually at the flat water symposium. The skills learnt from flat water freestyle – precise boat control and awareness – can be transferred to whitewater paddling. Many good freestyle canoeists are also good whitewater paddlers.

ADVENTURE

An afternoon spent exploring your local area is a fun and rewarding experience; it is also good practice for longer journeys in remote areas.

The open canoe was invented for journeying, to transport people and cargo on rivers and lakes and to hunt, trade and explore the world in which we live. Fast forward to the present day and the open canoe is still the ideal vehicle to discover the rivers and lakes of planet Earth. Humans are curious by nature and many of us relish the opportunity to travel, explore and learn about the world in which we live. The open canoe is a very environmentally friendly vehicle for travelling across water and is relatively easy to carry over land. With a canoe you can access places that very few other people can reach, watch birds and animals that would be scared off by motorised transport and keep yourself fit and healthy.

Planning and preparation

Choosing where to go is the first step when planning any canoeing journey. Choose a journey that is appropriate to your experience: the aim is to enjoy yourself, not to push yourself to the limits of survival. When is the best time of year to go on your adventure? Considering seasonal variation is important when planning an adventure. In the winter it may be too cold to paddle or the river may even be frozen; in spring there may be too much water in the river for a safe and controlled descent; in summer mosquitoes may be a danger and in autumn there may be too little water to paddle.

The journey to the put-in can be just as exciting and challenging as the descent of the river itself. No amount of planning will prepare you for the unexpected; sit down, stay calm and form a new plan.

'Shuttle' is the term used to describe transporting yourself and equipment to the put-in, from the take-out back to the put-in or from the take-out back to your base camp or home. This can often be the most complicated part of the planning, as transporting canoes can be challenging. For a local river trip, a simple car shuttle will suffice. Meet at the put-in, unload all the equipment, drive to the take-out with two cars and then return to the put-in with one car. For a two-week long journey across the Great Lakes of Canada, a more imaginative shuttle will be needed to get yourself and your equipment back to the outfitter. Shuttle a vehicle to the take-out, fly with a float plane from the take-out to the put-in and then paddle back to the take-out and the vehicles.

Time spent reading guidebooks and studying maps before the adventure will give you the best chance of comfortably achieving your goal.

Route planning

Once you have decided where you want to go, you will be able to plan your route. The start of all planning should involve looking at a large-scale map of the area in which you intend to explore and any relevant guidebooks and other sources of information on the area. The internet is a superb source of information; the world's biggest library is at your finger tips. Plan escape routes from your journey in case you need to head for safety. There are many situations where it may be necessary to abandon your plan; planning

these routes to safety in advance will save time in an emergency situation. That said, in many situations the quickest way to safety is to head at full speed to the take-out.

Food

Choosing the correct expedition food can mean the difference between success and failure. The active body needs over 2,500 calories per day, so when planning your expedition menu use the calorific information on the packaging to decide on the amounts of different foods to include.

There is no need to eat boil-in-the-bag meals day after day. Indeed, eating good food is important for both health and motivation. Pack as much fresh fruit and vegetables as possible, and use ingredients that can be combined to produce different meals according to your mood and that of the weather. Here are some examples.

Pancakes for breakfast: pancakes are easy to prepare when out and about and provide a welcome change from porridge for a hot breakfast.

Breakfast

Pancakes with banana, honey or chocolate spread (or all three together!) and tea, coffee or hot chocolate.

A good breakfast is essential before a day's paddling and is easy to prepare. First get up and boil a pot of water for a hot drink. Pancakes from an instant mix are quick, easy and tasty.

Lunch and daytime snacks

Pitta breads with cream cheese, ham, tomato; some bananas, apples or oranges; jelly babies; muesli bars; fruit and nut mix; and plenty of water.

A picnic lunch is a quick and easy way to stock up on energy halfway through the day. If you like a hot drink with your lunch, making a flask of hot water during breakfast is much more efficient than boiling water during your lunch stop. High energy snacks such as muesli bars and jelly babies will help keep your energy levels up between meals and can be a superb motivation booster when the going gets tough.

Dinner

Spaghetti carbonara with tea, coffee or hot chocolate and then a desert of toasted marshmallows.

As soon as you get into camp get the stove going and boil water for a hot drink. Spaghetti carbonara is a quick and easy meal to cook outdoors. Boil the spaghetti in a large pot. While it is cooking, mix cream and egg yolks together, then add ground pepper and parmesan cheese. Once the spaghetti is cooked, add the sauce to the pot with the spaghetti and stir. Fry some bacon lardons in another pan and then add them to the spaghetti. Hey presto! Dinner in 15 minutes. You can prepare the sauce at home and carry it in a wide-mouthed bottle to avoid the complexity of carrying eggs. Marshmallows around a camp fire are a perfect way to finish off a day outdoors.

Sitting around a campfire of an evening is the perfect end to a day's paddling. The warm light of the fire spreads a happy glow on all.

A combination of a wood stove and a multi-fuel stove being used to cook the evening meal. The multi-fuel stove is more suited to simmering vegetables and the wood stove is more fun for roasting sausages.

Cooking

A hot meal is always well received after a long day on the river and goes a long way towards boosting the motivation of a tired group. There are two options for cooking while on expedition: using a stove or cooking over an open fire. Relying on an open fire for cooking can be a risky plan. In many places open fires are forbidden, and it can be very tricky to light a fire when it is raining or after rain when everything is wet and sometimes there is just no wood to be found. A stove is a much more reliable method of cooking. An expedition stove should be efficient and reliable, lightweight and simple to use.

Outdoor cooking is a challenge to enjoy. Freshly caught fish over a camp fire is one of the greatest pleasures of expedition paddling.

Stoves come in a wide variety of shapes and sizes. One of the main differences to consider is the type of fuel the stove needs, as not all fuels are available in all places. Methylated spirits and

After every meal it is important to wash up. Keeping pots and pans clean will help prevent illness.

gas canisters can be tricky to find in many parts of the world. A multi-fuel stove, one that can burn most flammable liquids under pressure, is the best choice for expedition use. Before setting off, fire your stove up to check it is in good working order and that you have the correct fuel and fuel bottle. There is nothing worse than reaching your first camp and not being able to cook because your stove will not light.

To complement the stove, you will need pots and pans and other eating and cooking accessories. A set of two cooking pots with a lid will allow you to cook most camp meals satisfactorily. A fork, spoon, sharp knife and a thermal cup will complete your expedition cutlery and crockery. Don't forget to pack a scrubby brush and a drying-up cloth to wash up after meal time.

Water

Clean drinking water is an essential for all journeys, whether they last a few hours or weeks. For short journeys the solution is simple: fill up a bottle or hydration pack at home. If your journey is along an often-travelled waterway or you are planning to stay at campsites every night, you will be able to refill your water supplies on a daily basis from a source of clean water.

On a wilderness expedition, or when travelling through developing countries, the opportunity to find clean water from the tap is rare. There are three ways to prepare suspect water for drinking, cooking or washing when on expedition.

Boiling water for at least five minutes will kill bacteria. If the water is visibly dirty, it should be filtered through a paper coffee filter or cotton T shirt to remove the visible impurities before boiling. Before drinking boiled water it should be cooled in a sterile environment: a water bottle with the lid on is ideal. The major advantage of boiling water to purify it is that it requires very little extra equipment. You need only a pan or kettle and a source of heat, both of which you will need for cooking. The major disadvantage of boiling is that is takes time and energy to boil enough water for several people for just one day.

Iodine and water purification tablets are a quick and easy method of purifying water. Simply add the correct amount of liquid or tablets to the water and wait. During your expedition planning you will need to work out how much clean water you will need for your journey and pack the correct amount of iodine or tablets. Extra should also be carried in case of emergencies. Iodine and tablet-treated water does not taste the same as mineral water – it is a little like drinking from a swimming pool. If you can't stand the taste, pack powder flavouring for water or flavoured soluble vitamin tablets.

Sadly not all rivers are clean enough to drink from. If you want to drink directly from the river be sure that the water is clean; an upset stomach can quickly ruin an adventure.

The third option for cleaning water is to use a water filter system. Water filters are available in a huge variety of shapes and sizes to suit either individuals or groups. Filtering your water using a good quality filter is one of the most reliable ways of purifying suspect water while on expedition. Easy to carry and long lasting, a water filter is a practical alternative to boiling or using iodine or purification tablets. Good water filters are expensive; care must be taken not to clog the filtration system when filtering water from a source with a lot of sediment in.

Clean water is needed for much more than just drinking. If you suspect the water to be contaminated, it should be cleaned or purified before washing your hands, brushing your teeth or cleaning fruit and vegetables. A source of clean water is essential for all journeys; humans can last days without food but can become dehydrated very quickly.

Clothing

Thermals can be worn on the water and at camp. Lightweight, quick drying and warmth are the priorities for expedition clothing.

Keeping warm and dry plays a large part in the enjoyment of an adventure. Don't be tempted to pack your whole wardrobe into dry bags; you need very little to survive comfortably. Canoeing clothing is ideal for wearing in the great outdoors. Thermals and fleeces will keep you warm, and the waterproof shell layer will protect you from bad weather as well as any rain jacket. This set of clothing will be your primary set; you will wear it during the day canoeing and probably during the evening at camp. There is no reason to change your outfit for dinner when on expedition. A second set of thermals and fleeces should be packed as emergency clothing. A woolly hat, a pair of shorts for fine weather and warm socks complete the list. Many expedition paddlers also pack a down jacket to wear in the evening; they can be packed very small, provide lots of warmth and weigh almost nothing.

Shelter

If you are planning a journey that takes longer than one day you will need to consider where to sleep. The options are endless, from riverside hotels to a bivvy shelter made from branches and leaves. The weather should play an important part in your decision, as it is important to get a good night's sleep. Roughing it a bit is part of an adventure; lying awake freezing cold, wet and tired is not. Most canoeists choose to camp when on expedition, either with a tent or under a tarp construction.

Tents suitable for backpacking are also suitable for canoeing expeditions; aim for a lightweight tent that can be put up quickly and easily if necessary. When selecting a spot to pitch your tent several points should be considered: choose a level piece of ground with no protruding tree roots or rocks; clear away any small branches or twigs; if you are expecting bad weather look for natural shelter to protect you from strong winds or rain and, if you want to pack your tent away dry in the morning, pitch it so it has direct light from the sunrise. Many canoeists pack a lightweight tarp to provide extra shelter in the event of bad weather, or as a simple shelter to sleep under when mild weather is expected.

PITCH YOUR TENTS AWAY FROM THE WATER'S EDGE. IF THE RIVER STARTS TO RISE OVERNIGHT, YOU HAVE TIME TO REACT BEFORE THE WATER REACHES YOUR TENT.

A simple tarp shelter built with raft oars and paddles: a tarp is sufficient to keep the morning dew off your sleeping bags and can also provide a shelter to eat under if the weather is bad.

Rivers can rise very quickly. Even if it is not raining where you are, a heavy rainstorm or dam release upstream can cause a sudden rise in the water level. When selecting a camping spot, choose one a metre or so above the water level to give yourself time to evacuate if the situation arises. Tie all the canoes together and to a tree or rock to prevent them floating off. Tidy the camp as much as possible before bed to maximise your chance of a quick getaway if necessary.

Hygiene

An invigorating way of keeping clean.

Hygiene is an important part of everyday life and should not be forgotten when on an open canoeing journey. Thorough personal and group hygiene will prevent illness and infection, and help the group to stay happy and healthy during the expedition. Top of the list for hygienic practice is washing your hands. Wash them before preparing and eating food and before washing your face or brushing your teeth. Brush your teeth twice a day and try to wash yourself as often as possible. On long journeys, your fleeces and thermals should also be washed.

A waterfall makes a superb natural shower; the force of fresh water thundering down on your body can be very refreshing after several day's paddling. In colder climates, a strip wash using a flannel and a bowl of warm water works wonders.

Pack a multipurpose biodegradable soap for washing hands, hair, clothes and cooking utensils. You can tip the dirty water or wash under a waterfall without worrying about the soap bubbles damaging the environment.

Brushing your teeth is an important part of your daily hygiene routine out and about in the wild.

Answering the call of nature in the great outdoors is slightly trickier than when at home. It is important that a few basic rules are adhered to, to prevent illness and to stop the wilderness from turning into an unpleasant place to be. The first rule is to walk away from your camp or lunch spot; about fifty metres should suffice. This will prevent the embarrassment of relieving yourself in front of others and keep smells away. Take a trowel with you to dig a small hole to bury your waste. Toilet paper should either be burnt there and then in the hole, or packed into an airtight bag and disposed of properly at the end of the expedition. Once finished, use a stick to stir the contents of your hole around to aid decomposition, and then fill the hole in. After each and every visit to the toilet you should wash your hands thoroughly with soap and clean water.

In some areas, restrictions govern what can and can't be left behind in the wilderness. In the Grand Canyon all human waste must be carried out; special toilets are constructed with plastic bags which are then sealed and carried with the group to the take-out. Although extreme, such rules help to keep areas of outstanding natural beauty unaffected by human influence, and should be adhered to strictly.

First aid

On any journey there is a possibility that somebody may get injured or ill. Good planning and putting safety first will reduce this risk, but the risk is still there and should be prepared for. The aim of first aid is to prevent the injury or illness from getting worse and to promote the recovery of the casualty. What type of first aid precautions you should take depends on where you are in the world. First aid can be divided into two categories: knowledge and equipment. There is no point in carrying medical equipment or drugs you do not know how to use or administer. The further away you travel from professional medical help, the more knowledge you will need.

A simple first aid kit should be just that: a few plasters and bandages, painkillers, tape and energy sweets.

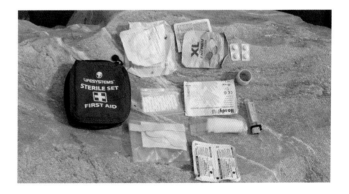

All canoeists should learn and regularly train in CPR (cardiopulmonary resuscitation); the danger of drowning is an ever-present

one for all canoeists. The first aid kit should be kept as simple as possible. The aim is not to perform surgery on the riverbank or to patch up an army.

For most minor injuries on a day trip, a plaster or tape can be applied and the casualty can carry on to the take-out. If the injury is such that paddling on is not possible, the option of walking out to the shuttle vehicle and then on to a hospital for professional assistance is recommended. If the injury is serious, then professional medical assistance should be arranged – a paramedic ambulance or helicopter should be called. Be sure you know the correct telephone number for the country in which you are travelling.

Many paddlers crave the peace and tranquillity of the wilderness. Be aware that the wilderness can be a very scary place for those who are unprepared to deal with accidents or illnesses.

For wilderness expeditions first aid takes on a whole new meaning. If you are days or weeks away from professional medical assistance, you should attend a wilderness first aid course and carry appropriate medical supplies to deal with the types of injuries and illnesses relevant to the country you are visiting.

Packing

Almost any type of canoe can be used for adventuring; the key is choosing the most appropriate canoe for your adventure. For a multi-day journey across lakes or along easy whitewater, a general purpose canoe will be ideal. For an extended self-supported journey, an expedition canoe with more carrying capacity is a good idea. For whitewater expeditions, a whitewater canoe will need to be adapted for you to carry sufficient equipment and supplies.

An expedition canoe (nearest) and a general purpose canoe. The expedition canoe has fuller ends and higher sides which allows more equipment to be loaded into the canoe.

This whitewater canoe has been fitted with special airbags that can be zipped open to allow equipment to be stored inside during the day. This solution maximises carrying capacity.

Once you have decided what equipment to take it must be packed into waterproof bags, known as dry bags. Expedition equipment can be divided into several groups: canoeing equipment, safety equipment, clothing, cooking and eating, and sleeping. Pack similar items together into smaller bags. The smaller bags are then packed into two large dry bags – one for items which will be needed at camp and the other for items which may be needed during the day while paddling. The camp bag will be the bigger of the two.

Pack the stove and cooking pans at the top so you will be able to boil water for a hot drink as soon as you reach camp. In the smaller dry bag include rescue kit, food for the day, repair kit and first aid kit. The first aid kit should be packed at the top of the bag where it can be easily accessed in the event of a medical emergency.

Aim to carry only essential items and assess each item for its worth and usefulness. As you become more experienced, you will be able to quickly and easily pack the items you need and leave behind those that are unnecessary.

Everything you take on your journey should be packed in dry bags. Pack logically, with the items you need most often on the top.

Ready to be packed into the canoe, the photograph on the left shows the camp equipment: tent, sleeping bag and food. The photograph on the right shows day kit, first aid kit, lunch and spare clothes, to be kept accessible in the canoe.

Suggested kit list (fine weather)

- Canoe

- Paddles

- Buoyancy aid

- Helmet, when whitewater is expected

- Throw bag, rescue rope and rescue kit

- Supportive shoes

- Thermal base layer top and bottom × 2

- Waterproof shell layer, top and bottom

- Lightweight shorts

- Camp shoes (flip flops)

- Down jacket

- Warm hat

- Warm socks × 2

- Thermarest or similar

- Sleeping bag

- Tent, bivvy bag or tarp

- Stove and fuel

- Lightweight pan set

- Sharp knife, fork, spoon, flask and insulated mug

- Food

- Water bottle and water filter

- First aid kit and repair kit

- Head torch and spare batteries and bulb

- Toothbrush, biodegradable soap and towel

- Map, route card, guide book, compass, GPS

- Mobile or satellite phone

- Sunglasses and sun cream

- Camera, spare batteries and memory cards

Loading the canoe

Once all the equipment is packed into dry bags, these bags must be packed into the canoe. When loading the dry bags into the canoe, aim to keep the weight in the centre of the canoe to avoid adversely affecting the trim.

Pack the dry bags into the middle of the canoe and distribute the weight evenly so that the canoe floats level in the water.

When journeying on calm water with a low risk of capsizing, it is not necessary to lash the dry bags into the canoe. If the canoe does capsize, it will be much easier to rescue without the added weight of the dry bags and the risk of them floating off during the rescue is minimal. For all other situations, the dry bags should be securely lashed into the canoe; simply clipping them onto the thwart will not do. Use straps or rope to lash the dry bags down to D rings glued to the hull of the canoe. Properly lashed down dry bags should not move around and will provide extra buoyancy in the event of a capsize, thus aiding your rescuers to quickly recover the canoe.

Navigation

Knowing where you are and in which direction to go is important for the success of any expedition or journey, whether an afternoon cruise on your local river or an exploratory expedition deep in the middle of somewhere.

Keep track of your progress on the map. Knowing where you are prevents you from becoming lost.

When paddling, keep the map close to hand. You may need to confirm your position in relation to a camping spot or a potential hazard such as a rapid. A compass and GPS are not essential for daytime navigating on a river, but are both very useful if you need to paddle in the dark, across a wide lake or in fog. If you lose or destroy your canoe, a map, compass and GPS will help you find the best route to safety on foot.

Pack your map into a waterproof map case, as wet maps are very difficult to use. If you choose a laminated map be aware that laminated things do not float very well. If it falls into the river, rescue it quick!

Portaging

Every once in a while, whether planned or not, you will have to carry your canoe and your equipment over land. Portaging is generally assumed to be a tiresome task but there are a few tips that can make the walk a little easier. The key to good portaging starts at the planning phase of your journey. A guidebook or map should give you an idea whether to expect portages on your journey, and how long they will be. If a journey is going to feature several long portages, pack as lightly as possible so you will only have to carry absolutely essential items along the portage trail.

Before carrying your canoe along the portage trail, first walk the trail carrying your bags and paddles. This enables you to scout the trail before walking through with your canoe. Once you have decided on a good route to carry your canoe, decide on the carrying technique to use: a double carry, a single carry or a portage trolley. Over flat even ground, using a portage trolley is by far the easiest and least energy sapping method of portaging an open canoe. Over uneven ground, a solo portage using the portage yoke is often easier. For extremely uneven terrain, dragging and lowering with ropes may be necessary.

Carry your bags and paddles along the portage trail first to find the easiest way to carry the canoe through on the second journey. A portage trolley helps to make light work of transporting a canoe over land.

Portaging takes time and energy; this should be factored into your planning. A simple portage of 500 metres will require you to walk 1.5 kilometres. First you walk the portage with your bags, then back and then a second time with your canoe. When portaging over uneven ground or near the water, wear your buoyancy aid and helmet to protect you in the event of a fall. Another useful piece of advice is to take your time.

Playing safe

When on expedition take your safety extra seriously. Wear a helmet even when paddling small rapids; a head injury can threaten the safety of the whole group.

When on expedition, days away from help or civilisation, extra care should be taken to protect yourself and your equipment. Injuries and broken equipment are much harder to deal with without outside help. This may mean being cautious and portaging a rapid you would have otherwise paddled, e.g. if you had come across it on a day paddle, where the consequences of losing or damaging your canoe are less life-threatening. When your goal is still several hundred kilometres away and the easiest way of reaching it is with your canoe, you should protect your mode of transport and the food and accommodation that is packed into it.

*The world is a beautiful
place; take care of it
and enjoy it safely.*

INDEX

Venture Canoes®

Explore the water

"Venture have opened up Canoeing to a wider world – brilliant designs in tough durable materials that are light, but affordable and accessible to more people than ever before." Bob Timms - BCU Level 5 coach